# TEACHER'S PET PUBLICATIONS

## LITPLAN TEACHER PACK
for
Native Son
based on the book by
Richard Wright

Written by
Mary B. Collins

© 1996 Teacher's Pet Publications
All Rights Reserved

This **LitPlan** for Richard Wright's
*Native Son*
has been brought to you by Teacher's Pet Publications, Inc.

Copyright Teacher's Pet Publications 1996
11504 Hammock Point
Berlin MD 21811

Only the student materials in this unit plan (such as worksheets,
study questions, and tests) may be reproduced multiple times
for use in the purchaser's classroom.

For any additional copyright questions,
contact Teacher's Pet Publications.

www.tpet.com

# TABLE OF CONTENTS - *Native Son*

| | |
|---|---|
| Introduction | 5 |
| Unit Objectives | 7 |
| Reading Assignment Sheet | 8 |
| Unit Outline | 9 |
| Study Questions (Short Answer) | 13 |
| Quiz/Study Questions (Multiple Choice) | 21 |
| Pre-reading Vocabulary Worksheets | 33 |
| Lesson One (Introductory Lesson) | 47 |
| Nonfiction Assignment Sheet | 49 |
| Oral Reading Evaluation Form | 53 |
| Writing Assignment 1 | 55 |
| Writing Assignment 2 | 62 |
| Writing Assignment 3 | 64 |
| Writing Evaluation Form | 65 |
| Vocabulary Review Activities | 59 |
| Extra Writing Assignments/Discussion ?s | 57 |
| Unit Review Activities | 66 |
| Unit Tests | 69 |
| Unit Resource Materials | 101 |
| Vocabulary Resource Materials | 115 |

# A FEW NOTES ABOUT THE AUTHOR
## Richard Wright

WRIGHT, Richard (1908-1960). The American author Richard Wright pictured with brutal realism what it meant to be black in a white society. His writings speak with the raw voice of an anguish not often evident in novels.

Richard Nathaniel Wright was born on Sept. 4, 1908, on a plantation near Natchez, Mississippi. His father was a mill hand, and his mother taught in a country school. Young Wright's childhood was generally one of poverty, frustration, and despair. When he was 5, his father left the family, and when he was not yet 10, his mother became paralyzed. He was sent to live with relatives. At 15 he left home and for several years drifted from one city to another, working at whatever jobs he could find. In Chicago he worked nights in the post office. Days he spent reading and writing. During the depression of the 1930's, he lost his job and had to go on relief. Not long afterward he joined the Communist party, as did thousands of other young Americans at the time.

In 1937 Wright moved to New York City, where he worked on a Fereral Writers' Project. His first published book, *Uncle Tom's Children*, appeared in 1938. It was a collection of four stories dealing with racial prejudice and violence in the South. But it was Wright's novel *Native Son* (1940) that brought him world fame. This powerful story of a Chicago black driven to crime was made into a play by Wright and Paul Green. It was successfully staged in 1941.

Wright's first marriage--to a ballet dancer--ended in divorce. In 1941 he married Ellen Poplar of New York City, and they had two daughters. Wright became increasingly disillusioned with the Communist party and finally left it. In 1945 he published *Black Boy*, an autobiography of his childhood and youth. It confirmed him as a major American writer.

His discontent with American society persisted. As a youth he had experienced not only hardship but vicious racial prejudice as well, and as a man he continued to encounter it. In 1946 he and his white wife left the United States to live in Paris.

Wright wrote several novels during the next 14 years, but they were not well received. He also wrote some travel books and other nonfiction. On November 28, 1960, he died in Paris of a heart attack.

---- Courtesy of Compton's Learning Company

# INTRODUCTION

This unit has been designed to develop students' reading, writing, thinking, and language skills through exercises and activities related to *Native Son* by Richard Wright. It includes eighteen lessons, supported by extra resource materials.

The **introductory lesson** introduces students to some background to the novel through a bulletin board activity. Following the introductory activity, students are given a transition to explain how the activity relates to the book they are about to read. Following the transition, students are given the materials they will be using during the unit. At the end of the lesson, students begin the pre-reading work for the first reading assignment.

The **reading assignments** are done by "book" divisions (Book One: Fear, Book Two: Flight, Book Three: Fate). Students have approximately 20 minutes of pre-reading work to do prior to each reading assignment. This pre-reading work involves reviewing the study questions for the assignment and doing some vocabulary work for 8 to 10 vocabulary words they will encounter in their reading.

The **study guide questions** are fact-based questions; students can find the answers to these questions right in the text. These questions come in two formats: short answer or multiple choice. The best use of these materials is probably to use the short answer version of the questions as study guides for students (since answers will be more complete), and to use the multiple choice version for occasional quizzes. If your school has the appropriate machinery, it might be a good idea to make transparencies of your answer keys for the overhead projector.

The **vocabulary work** is intended to enrich students' vocabularies as well as to aid in the students' understanding of the book. Prior to each reading assignment, students will complete a two-part worksheet for approximately 8 to 10 vocabulary words in the upcoming reading assignment. Part I focuses on students' use of general knowledge and contextual clues by giving the sentence in which the word appears in the text. Students are then to write down what they think the words mean based on the words' usage. Part II nails down the definitions of the words by giving students dictionary definitions of the words and having students match the words to the correct definitions based on the words' contextual usage. Students should then have an understanding of the words when they meet them in the text.

After each reading assignment, students will go back and formulate answers for the study guide questions. Discussion of these questions serves as a **review** of the most important events and ideas presented in the reading assignments.

After students complete reading the work, there is a **vocabulary review** lesson which pulls together all of the fragmented vocabulary lists for the reading assignments and gives students a review of all of the words they have studied.

A lesson is devoted to the **extra discussion questions/writing assignments**. These questions focus on interpretation, critical analysis and personal response, employing a variety of thinking skills and adding to the students' understanding of the novel.

There is a **group activity** in which students work in small groups to discuss symbolism, imagery and themes from the novel.

The group activity is followed by a **reports and discussion** session in which the groups share their ideas about the themes with the entire class; thus, the entire class is exposed to information about all of the themes and the entire class can discuss each theme based on the nucleus of information brought forth by each of the groups.

There are three **writing assignments** in this unit, each with the purpose of informing, persuading, or having students express personal opinions. The first assignment is to inform: students explain how the title of the first "book" (Fear) is appropriate. The second assignment is to express personal opinions: students will have read several articles related to the ideas presented in the novel. They will review their notes and write a composition explaining their own ideas about the topic of their research. The third assignment is to persuade: students persuade you that Bigger's sentence was (or was not) "just"; he did or did not get what he deserved.

In addition, there is a **nonfiction reading assignment project**. Students are required to read five different nonfiction articles related in some way to *Native Son*. After reading their nonfiction pieces, students will fill out a worksheet on which they answer questions regarding facts, interpretation, criticism, and personal opinions. During one class period, students make **oral presentations** about the nonfiction pieces they have read. This not only exposes all students to a wealth of information, it also gives students the opportunity to practice **public speaking**.

The **review lesson** pulls together all of the aspects of the unit. The teacher is given four or five choices of activities or games to use which all serve the same basic function of reviewing all of the information presented in the unit.

The **unit test** comes in two formats: multiple choice or short answer. As a convenience, two different tests for each format have been included. There is also an advanced short answer test for students who need more of a challenge.

There are additional **support materials** included with this unit. The **resource sections** include suggestions for an in-class library, crossword and word search puzzles related to the novel, and extra vocabulary worksheets. There is a list of **bulletin board ideas** which gives the teacher suggestions for bulletin boards to go along with this unit. In addition, there is a list of **extra class activities** the teacher could choose from to enhance the unit or as a substitution for an exercise the teacher might feel is inappropriate for his/her class. **Answer keys** are located directly after the **reproducible student materials** throughout the unit. Only the student materials may be reproduced for use in the teacher's classroom without infringement of copyrights.

# UNIT OBJECTIVES - *Native Son*

1. Through reading *Native Son* students will gain a better understanding of racial issues facing Americans.

2. Students will demonstrate their understanding of the text on four levels: factual, interpretive, critical and personal.

3. Students will consider the central themes of the book: a. The plight of the black man; that is, the inherent problems a black person had/has in our society   b. The idea of seeing a person as *a person* rather than a *black* person or a *white* person c. How we face and attempt to overcome racial prejudice  d. The influence of Communism in America  e. The functioning of our criminal justice system relating to racial issues

4. Students will be given the opportunity to practice reading aloud and silently to improve their skills in each area.

5. Students will answer questions to demonstrate their knowledge and understanding of the main events and characters in *Native Son* as they relate to the author's theme development.

6. Students will enrich their vocabularies and improve their understanding of the novel through the vocabulary lessons prepared for use in conjunction with the novel.

7. The writing assignments in this unit are geared to several purposes:
    a. To have students demonstrate their abilities to inform, to persuade, or to express their own personal ideas
        Note:  Students will demonstrate ability to write effectively to <u>inform</u> by developing and organizing facts to convey information. Students will demonstrate the ability to write effectively to <u>persuade</u> by selecting and organizing relevant information, establishing an argumentative purpose, and by designing an appropriate strategy for an identified audience. Students will demonstrate the ability to write effectively to <u>express personal ideas</u> by selecting a form and its appropriate elements.
    b. To check the students' reading comprehension
    c. To make students think about the ideas presented by the novel
    d. To encourage logical thinking
    e. To provide an opportunity to practice good grammar and improve students' use of the English language.

8. Students will read aloud, report, and participate in large and small group discussions to improve their public speaking and personal interaction skills.

# READING ASSIGNMENT SHEET - *Native Son*

| Date Assigned | Assignment | Completion Date |
|---|---|---|
|  | Book One: Fear |  |
|  | Book Two: Flight |  |
|  | Book Three: Fate |  |

# UNIT OUTLINE - *Native Son*

| 1<br><br>Introduction | 2<br><br>PVR Book One | 3<br><br>Project/Library | 4<br><br>Study ?s Book One<br>PVR Book Two | 5<br><br>Read Book Two |
|---|---|---|---|---|
| 6<br><br>Writing Assignment #1 | 7<br><br>Study ?s Book Two<br>PVR Book Three | 8<br><br>Read Book Three | 9<br><br>Study ?s Book Three<br><br>Extra Questions | 10<br><br>Vocabulary |
| 11<br><br>Writing Assignment #2 | 12<br><br>Group Activity | 13<br><br>Group Reports & Discussion | 14<br><br>Nonfiction Reports | 15<br><br>Nonfiction Reports |
| 16<br><br>Writing Assignment #3 | 17<br><br>Review | 18<br><br>Test | | |

P=Preview Study Questions  V=Prereading Vocabulary Worksheets  R=Read

# STUDY GUIDE QUESTIONS

# SHORT ANSWER STUDY GUIDE QUESTIONS - *Native Son*

Book One: Fear
1. Describe Bigger's relationship with his family.
2. What does Bigger mean when he says, "Half the time I feel like I'm on the outside of the world peeping in through a knot-hole in the fence. . ."?
3. Why do you think Wright included the scene with the sky-writing airplane?
4. What is Bigger saying when he tells Gus that white folks live "Right down here in my stomach"?
5. What are the two controlling emotions in Bigger's life?
6. Who is going to rob Blum's store?
7. Why isn't the robbery carried out?
8. How do Jack and G.H. react to Bigger's attack on Gus?
9. What causes Bigger to lose his temper again?
10. Do Jan and Mary see Bigger as a man?
11. Why can't Bigger speak to Mrs. Dalton when she enters Mary's room?
12. How and why does Bigger kill Mary? What does he do with the body? Why?
13. How does Bigger feel after killing Mary?
14. Why can Bigger fall asleep so easily after committing such horrible acts?

Book Two: Flight
1. Why is Bigger no longer fearful in the presence of Gus, Jack and G.H.?
2. To what is Wright referring when he writes, ". . . they were a sort of a great natural force, like a stormy sky looming overhead, or like a deep swirling river stretching suddenly at one's feet in the dark"?
3. Who is Bessie?
4. How does Bigger respond to Britten's interrogation?
5. Why does Bigger threaten Jan with a gun?
6. What is Bigger's plan to get money from Mr. Dalton?
7. How is the ransom money to be delivered?
8. Why does Britten question Peggy?
9. Why are some of Britten's questions to Peggy concerning Bigger a bit ridiculous?
10. What is Bigger's downfall?
11. Why had Bigger not cleaned the furnace before?
12. Why does Bigger kill Bessie?
13. How does Bigger rationalize to himself that Mary and Bessie were responsible for their own deaths?
14. How do the men finally capture Bigger?

*Native Son* Short Answer Study Guide Page 2

Book Three: Fate
1. Who is Bigger's first visitor?
2. Why does Bigger reject the pleas of Rev. Hammond?
3. How does Bigger view Jan during the visit at the inquest?
4. How does Mr. Dalton show that his "heart is not bitter" towards Negro people?
5. Why do the ping-pong tables upset Max?
6. Why does the presence of Bigger's family and friends make him feel ashamed?
7. Why does Bigger think, "They ought to be glad!"?
8. Why does Buckley try to get Bigger to admit that Jan was involved?
9. How does Buckley manipulate Bigger?
10. Why is Bessie's body put on exhibition at the inquest?
11. Where do the police and reporters take Bigger after the inquest? Why?
12. Does Max really understand Bigger's feelings?
13. How does Bigger feel after the conversation with Max?
14. Why does Bigger become fearful after speaking to Max?
15. What had Bigger felt and caught a glimpse of for the first time in his life?
16. For what does Max plead?
17. Does Max ever understand Bigger?

STUDY GUIDE QUESTIONS - *Native Son*
Short Answer Format Answer Key

Book One: Fear

1. Describe Bigger's relationship with his family.
    He is ashamed and resentful when he is with them. He is ashamed that they have nothing and he is powerless to help them, and he is resentful that they look to him for support.

2. What does Bigger mean when he says, "Half the time I feel like I'm on the outside of the world peeping in through a knot-hole in the fence. . ."?
    He means that although he lives in the world, somehow he is not a part of it at all. The world is beyond his grasp as well as his understanding. He feels a stranger and an alien in it.

3. Why do you think Wright included the scene with the sky-writing airplane?
    He uses it to illustrate how the white man's world is unattainable to Bigger. Bigger sees the plane and comments that he would like to learn to fly, but that even the chance to try is denied him. The distant plane represents the distance between Bigger and the world of a decent job, home and life.

4. What is Bigger saying when he tells Gus that white folks live "Right down here in my stomach"?
    He is describing the ache and frustration bottled up inside of him from a life of being told where to live and what to do. He has, in effect, swallowed his hate and anger and it rages inside him.

5. What are the two controlling emotions in Bigger's life?
    "These were the rhythms of his life: indifference and violence . . . . moments of silence and moments of anger . . . ."

6. Who is going to rob Blum's store?
    Bigger, Gus, Jack and G.H. plan to rob it.

7. Why isn't the robbery carried out?
    Bigger physically attacks Gus when Gus arrives late at Doc's. He accuses Gus of being so late that it is too late to carry out the robbery. Actually, Bigger doesn't want to rob the store anymore, so the fight with Gus is a good way to delay and to vent his frustration caused by his own feelings of fear.

8. How do Jack and G.H. react to Bigger's attack on Gus?
    Initially they tell Bigger to leave Gus alone, but because they are frightened of his temper they do not strongly insist. They eventually begin to laugh and enjoy the spectacle when they realize that Bigger has made his point and will let Gus go.

9. What causes Bigger to lose his temper again?
>   Gus throws a pool ball, hitting Bigger in the wrist. Bigger lunges after Gus but slips on a cue stick left on the floor. Jack and G.H. laugh at this turn in events, and Bigger's rage and embarrassment boil over.

10. Do Jan and Mary see Bigger as a man?
>   No, they both believe in equality and freedom for all people, but they don't look at Bigger as an individual man; to them he is a Negro man, not just a man. Their treatment of Bigger, while superficially friendly, is actually very unkind. they can see that Bigger is uneasy around them, and yet they force him to stay in the front seat between them and to eat with them. They cannot see that Bigger is trapped by their desire to treat him nice just as he is trapped by other white people's desire to abuse him.

11. Why can't Bigger speak to Mrs. Dalton when she enters Mary's room?
>   He is terrified. He is in a rich, white girl's bedroom, and she is drunk. Bigger knows he could never explain the situation, that he would most likely be accused of rape, at least. He knows that the punishment for raping a white woman is death.

12. How and why does Bigger kill Mary? What does he do with the body? Why?
>   He puts the pillow over her face in an effort to keep her quiet so Mrs. Dalton will go away and not discover him. However, he has the pillow there for quite some time, and Mary suffocates. He cannot leave the body as evidence, so he puts it in the trunk, carries it to the furnace room, and puts it into the furnace.

13. How does Bigger feel after killing Mary?
>   He is still scared because now he is really in trouble with the white man's world, but he also feels a kind of pride and a direction for his life, for the first time in his life.

14. Why can Bigger fall asleep so easily after committing such horrible acts?
>   He is totally exhausted, and although he realizes the acts were horrible, he feels a sense of relief that his life has a direction and that some of his violent frustrations have been vented.

<u>Book Two: Flight</u>
1. Why is Bigger no longer fearful in the presence of Gus, Jack and G.H.?
>   Bigger no longer fears them because the murder of Mary has given him a sense of pride. They were afraid to rob a white man, but he has killed a white girl. For the first time in his life, Bigger actually feels "bigger" and in control. Notice how he doles out the little gifts of cigarettes and money to the gang, and also notice that they show him a respect not born of fearing his temper but of being almost in awe of his new purpose and command.

2. To what is Wright referring when he writes, ". . . they were a sort of a great natural force, like a stormy sky looming overhead, or like a deep swirling river stretching suddenly at one's feet in the dark"?

   He is describing how black people see white people less as people and more like a great natural force as uncontrollable as the weather.

3. Who is Bessie?

   She is Bigger's girlfriend.

4. How does Bigger respond to Britten's interrogation?

   For the first time in his life, Bigger reacts towards a white man by thinking instead of fearing. Notice in response to Britten's questions Bigger does not feel the burning heat of fear but remains calm and thoughtful. Bigger sticks to his story, and Britten comes away more interested in Jan, just as Bigger wants him to be.

5. Why does Bigger threaten Jan with a gun?

   Jan is confused and wants Bigger to talk to him, but Bigger is overwhelmed with guilt because he has lied about Jan (someone who has tried to be nice to him). Not wanting to face Jan's questions and feeling guilty, Bigger reacts by threatening Jan with a gun.

6. What is Bigger's plan to get money from Mr. Dalton?

   He is going to send a ransom note to the Daltons demanding $10,000. He will sign the note "Red" to make the Daltons think their daughter was kidnapped by the communists.

7. How is the ransom money to be delivered?

   It is to be thrown from a moving car onto the sidewalk. Bessie will be watching from a deserted building and will pick up the money when the car has disappeared.

8. Why does Britten question Peggy?

   He is trying to find out if Bigger has any mannerisms which would suggest he might be a part of the communist party.

9. Why are some of Britten's questions to Peggy concerning Bigger a bit ridiculous?

   The political stereotypes Britten describes (such as waving hands) are as stupid as the racial stereotypes common at the time. Jan is a communist, yet he certainly wouldn't fit Britten's descriptions.

10. What is Bigger's downfall?

    The ashes in the furnace are. If Bigger had cleaned the ashes out when he first tried to, he would probably have gotten away with the crime.

11. Why had Bigger not cleaned the furnace before?

    Every time he tried to shake down the ashes or thought about cleaning them out of the furnace, he visualized Mary's bloody, severed head and became fearful again.

12. Why does Bigger kill Bessie?

    She is a threat to him. He could never escape with her because she is too upset and afraid. On the other hand, if he leaves her behind, she will tell the police everything. He sees no other course of action than to kill her.

13. How does Bigger rationalize to himself that Mary and Bessie were responsible for their own deaths?

    He thinks both girls should have left him alone. Mary made him promise to keep her secret and she got drunk, so he had to be the one to take her upstairs. Bessie kept nagging him to tell her what was wrong, making him tell her more than she should have known. They both forced him into a position where he had to kill them, he thought.

14. How do the men finally capture Bigger?

    They corner him on a water tower and turn the firehose on him, forcing him to surrender.

Book Three: Fate

1. Who is Bigger's first visitor?

    Reverend Hammond, the preacher from his mother's church, is his first visitor.

2. Why does Bigger reject the pleas of Rev. Hammond?

    Bigger has never been able to substitute the need to live in the world of men with a hope of an eternal afterlife. Bigger cannot accept that he must suffer in this world and patiently wait for death to bring happiness.

3. How does Bigger view Jan during the visit at the inquest?

    For the first time in his life, Bigger sees a white man as a human being and not as an object of fear or hate. Jan's speech to Bigger, admitting that he had been blind to Bigger's reality as a black man opens Bigger's eyes just as Bigger has opened Jan's eyes.

4. How does Mr. Dalton show that his "heart is not bitter" towards Negro people?

    He sends ping-pong tables to the South Side Boys' Club.

5. Why do the ping-pong tables upset Max?

    He wants Dalton to see that the oppressed people need a meaningful life, not ping-pong. He wants Dalton to recognize that the human needs and drives within him are present in all men, and that his material gestures do not help them endure the suppression of those human needs.

6. Why does the presence of Bigger's family and friends make him feel ashamed?
   He feels their presence exposes and enhances his weaknesses. He sees their shame and feels them wrap him in it.

7. Why does Bigger think, "They ought to be glad!"?
   Bigger thinks his friends and family should be able to feel a part of the freedom and elation he experienced by committing the murders and giving life to his fears and demons. The fact that they are totally blind to his brief experience of manhood and free-will makes him feel contempt for them.

8. Why does Buckley try to get Bigger to admit that Jan was involved?
   He does not believe a black man could think of and commit such a crime alone, and he wants to implicate the communists.

9. How does Buckley manipulate Bigger?
   He tells him he knows how bad it feels to be black, he accuses him of other rapes and murders, and he hints at sending Bigger to a mental hospital. He wears Bigger out to the point where he doesn't care anymore whether he lives or dies.

10. Why is Bessie's body put on exhibition at the inquest?
    The coroner wants to stir up hatred by showing the physical cruelty of which Bigger was capable. The fact that Bessie, a black woman, was killed was immaterial to them. Her body was used to help get a conviction against Bigger for killing a white woman.

11. Where do the police and reporters take Bigger after the inquest? Why?
    They take him to the Dalton residence and ask him to reenact the rape and murder of Mary, partly for their own amusement and partly because photos will sell papers.

12. Does Max really understand Bigger's feelings?
    No, he sees Bigger more as a victim of an oppressive, capitalistic society. Max does not hear the human needs that Bigger tries to express.

13. How does Bigger feel after the conversation with Max?
    He feels more relaxed than he has ever felt before, free of much of the strain and stress that has controlled him.

14. Why does Bigger become fearful after speaking to Max?
    He feels he has made himself vulnerable somehow and yet recognizes to a certain extent that he spoke to Max man-to-man without the barriers of hate and fear.

15. What had Bigger felt and caught a glimpse of for the first time in his life?
    He felt a connection with the rest of humanity.

16. For what does Max plead?
    He pleads for a life sentence for Bigger (as opposed to the death sentence the State requests).

17. Does Max ever understand Bigger?
    No, he doesn't. He sees a Negro boy caught up in the struggle of an oppressed life caused by the white, capitalistic society.

MULTIPLE CHOICE STUDY GUIDE/QUIZ QUESTIONS - *Native Son*

Book One: Fear
1. Describe Bigger's relationship with his family.
    A. He is ashamed that they have nothing and he is powerless to help them. He is resentful that they look to him for support.
    B. He is insecure because he thinks they don't like him. He feels worthless.
    C. He portrays an aura of confidence to make them feel better. He is especially loving towards his mother.
    D. He is angry that he still lives with them. He despised them, especially his sister.

2. How does Bigger feel about his place in the world?
    A. He is content, because he doesn't know any better.
    B. He is angry, and thinks the world owes him more.
    C. He feels he is a stranger and an alien in it.
    D. He thinks he has been put on the earth for a reason, and that things will improve.

3. How did Wright show the distance between the white man's world and Bigger's?
    A. He contrasts the white and black neighborhoods.
    B. He uses billboards to show that the ads are directed to the white population of the city.
    C. He contrasts the sun outside with the darkness of the pool room.
    D. He uses the sky writing airplane to show how the white man's world is unattainable.

4. How does Bigger explain his feelings about the white folks to Gus?
    A. He says they are all liars and cheats.
    B. He says they live in his stomach; he has swallowed his anger and frustration.
    C. He says they are like poison in his blood.
    D. He says they are buzzards, preying on the weaknesses of Blacks.

5. What are the two controlling emotions in Bigger's life?
    A. They are fear and frustration.
    B. They are bewilderment and confidence.
    C. They are indifference and violence.
    D. They are optimism and pessimism.

*Native Son* Multiple Choice Study Questions Page 2

6. Who is going to Rob Blum's store?
    A. Bigger, Jack, and Doc.
    B. Bigger, Jack, Gus, and G.H.
    C. Gus, Jack, Jan, and Bigger.
    D. G.H., Jack, Bigger, and Buddy.

7. Why isn't the robbery carried out?
    A. The police are patrolling the street and they back out at the last minute.
    B. It starts snowing. They think they might get caught if they leave footprints in the snow.
    C. Someone else in the pool hall overhears them talking and threatens to tell the police.
    D. Bigger physically attacks Gus when Gus arrives late at Doc's. he accuses Gus of being so late that it is too late to carry out their plans.

8. How do Jack and G.H. react to Bigger's attack on Gus?
    A. Initially they are frightened of Bigger's temper, but they enjoy the spectacle when they realize that Bigger will let Gus go.
    B. They ignore it because they don't want to get involved.
    C. They take Gus's side and subdue Bigger.
    D. They make a bet on who will win, and they watch but don't interfere.

9. What causes Bigger to lose his temper again?
    A. Doc throws a bucket of cold water on the two of them.
    B. The others call him a coward for not robbing the store.
    C. Jack and G.H. laugh at Bigger when he slips on a cue stick left on the floor.
    D. He plays a game of pool with the others and loses. It is too much for him to handle, and he explodes.

10. Do Jan and Mary see Bigger as a man?
    A. Yes, they do.
    B. No, they don't.

11. Does Bigger speak to Mrs. Dalton when she enters Mary's room?
    A. Yes, he tells her the whole story.
    B. No, he is too afraid that he could not explain the situation.

*Native Son* Multiple Choice Study Questions Page 3

12. How and why does Bigger kill Mary?
    A. He puts the pillow over her face to keep her quiet, and accidentally suffocates her.
    B. He decides to rob her and knifes her when she resists.
    C. He is still angry about having to eat with her and Jan, so he beats her to death.
    D. She threatens to tell her parents he attacked her, so he strangles her.

13. What does he do with the body?
    A. He puts it in the trunk of his car, drives the car to Jan's house and parks it out front, hoping to implicate Jan.
    B. He panics and leaves it in the bedroom. He thinks that whoever finds her will think she was drunk and accidentally suffocated herself.
    C. He puts it in the furnace. He hopes her parents will think she has gone on her trip already and won't discover her death for a while.
    D. He chops it up, puts it in her traveling trunk, and takes it to the dump.

14. How does Bigger feel after killing Mary?
    A. He is still scared because now he is really in trouble with the white man's world, but he also feels a kind of pride and a direction for his life.
    B. He is remorseful, but isn't sober enough yet to think about what to do next.
    C. He is ashamed of himself and terrified at what will happen if anyone finds out what he did.
    D. He feels totally evil, but strong. He is sure he will get away with the crime.

15. Bigger falls asleep easily after committing these horrible acts. Which of these is not one of the reasons that he is able to sleep?
    A. He is totally exhausted.
    B. He feels a sense of relief that his life now has a direction.
    C. He was so drunk that he doesn't remember anything. He thinks it was a dream.
    D. He has released some of his violent frustrations.

*Native Son* Multiple Choice Study Questions Page 4

Book Two: Flight

16. How does Bigger act in the presence of Gus, Jack, and G.H.?
    A. He acts the same way he always has. He doesn't want to arouse suspicions.
    B. He says he is too good for them, and he snubs them.
    C. He acts "white," and they resent it.
    D. He shows a new sense of command and purpose.

17. To what is Wright referring when he writes, "...they were a sort of a great natural force, like a stormy sky looming overhead, or like a deep swirling river stretching suddenly at one's feet in the dark."?
    A. He is describing good luck and bad luck.
    B. He is describing how black people see white people.
    C. He is describing Bigger's emotions.
    D. He is describing race relations in general.

18. Who is Bessie?
    A. She is Bigger's girlfriend.
    B. She is the maid at the Dalton's home.
    C. She is one of Mary's friends, who has now befriended Bigger.
    D. She is Bigger's sister.

19. How does Bigger respond to Britten's interrogation?
    A. He refuses to speak.
    B. He reacts by thinking instead of fearing. He sticks to his story.
    C. He threatens Britten and uses foul language to try to intimidate him.
    D. He pretends he doesn't understand what Britten is talking about.

20. Why does Bigger threaten Jan with a gun?
    A. Bigger wants Jan to feel intimidated so he won't ask any more questions.
    B. Bigger intends to kill Jan, but stops himself at the last minute.
    C. Bigger is angry. He thinks the whole mess in Jan's fault, and wants to make Jan realize it, too.
    d. Bigger is overwhelmed with guilt at lying about Jan, and doesn't want to face Jan's questions.

*Native Son* Multiple Choice Study Questions Page 5

21. What is Bigger's plan to get money from Mr. Dalton?
    A. He plans to act like a model worker, hoping Mr. Dalton will notice and give him a raise.
    B. He pretends that Jan has offered him money to keep quiet, in the hopes that Mr. Dalton will offer even more money if he talks.
    C. He is going to send a ransom note to the Daltons and sign it "Red" to make them think Mary was kidnapped by the communists.
    D. He pawns the jewelry he had taken from Mary's body before he killed her.

22. Who is his accomplice in this scheme?
    A. Buddy
    B. Bessie
    C. Jan
    D. No one. He works alone.

23. Why does Britten question Peggy?
    A. He wants to know if she heard any suspicious noises the night Mary came home late.
    B. He suspects that she may be an accomplice in some sort of plot involving Mary.
    C. He is trying to find out if Bigger might be a part of the communist party.
    D. He thinks she looks shifty, and may be hiding something.

24. How does Wright portray some of the questions Britten asks?
    A. They are insightful.
    B. They are unrealistic.
    C. They are symbolic of the plight of the Black man in society.
    D. They are ridiculous political stereotypes.

25. What is Bigger's downfall?
    A. The ashes in the furnace are. If he had cleaned the furnace out when he first tried to, he probably would have gotten away with the crime.
    B. The ransom note is. The police were able to match it to a writing sample from his application for work with Mr. Dalton.
    C. His own bragging is. He boasted so much to his friends at the pool hall and waved his roll of money around so much that they became suspicious.
    D. His concern for Jan is. He finds that he is not able to implicate an innocent man, especially one who had been nice to him.

*Native Son* Multiple Choice Study Questions Page 6

26. What does Bigger do when Mary's bones are discovered?
    A. He immediately accuses Jan of concealing the body.
    B. He sneaks out of the room and runs away.
    C. He breaks down and confesses everything.
    D. He insists they are animal bones. He tells the others that he had accidentally hit a dog with the car, and brought it to the furnace to get rid of it.

27. What does Bigger do about Bessie?
    A. He gives her money and promises to send her more as long as she keeps quiet.
    B. He leaves without telling her anything.
    C. He kills her because she is too much of a threat to him.
    D. He forces her to marry him, so that she will stay with him. In the event they are caught, she will not be able to testify against him.

28. How does Bigger deal with his actions with regards to Mary and Bessie?
    A. He prays for forgiveness, because he knows he has done terrible wrongs.
    B. He blocks both incidents from his mind so completely that he does not remember what he did.
    C. He blames them on drinking and tells himself he is not responsible for what he does when he is drunk.
    D. He thinks both women forced him into a position where he had to do what he did.

29. How do the men finally capture Bigger?
    A. They set food out in a few of the empty buildings. He is so hungry that he cannot resist eating, and he is captured.
    B. They threaten to imprison his family if he does not give himself up.
    C. They corner him on a water tower and turn the firehose on him, forcing him to surrender.
    D. They pretend to call off the search, and even announce it in the newspaper. When Bigger tries to leave the city a few days later, the undercover agents capture him.

*Native Son* Multiple Choice Study Questions Page 7

Book Three: Fate

30. Who is Bigger's first visitor?
    A. Reverend Hammond, the preacher from his mother's church, is his first visitor.
    B. Mr. Dalton is his first visitor.
    C. His mother is his first visitor.
    D. A court appointed psychiatrist is his first visitor.

31. Why does Bigger reject the pleas of Reverend Hammond?
    A. He doesn't believe he is worth saving.
    B. He thinks if he does as the Reverend asks he will be admitting his guilt, and may get a harsher sentence.
    C. He cannot accept that he must suffer in this world and patiently wait for death to bring happiness.
    D. He doesn't believe in God at all.

32. How does Bigger view Jan during the visit at the inquest?
    A. He sees Jan as a nuisance.
    B. He sees Jan as a human being and not as an object of fear or hate.
    C. He sees Jan as the reason for all of his troubles.
    D. He sees Jan as his only possible hope of salvation, and begs him for help.

33. How does Mr. Dalton show that his "heart is not bitter" towards Negro people?
    A. He has Bigger's family brought to see him in a private car.
    B. He sends ping-pong tables to the South Side Boys' Club.
    C. He takes out a full page ad in the newspaper and make a statement to that effect.
    D. He sends Bigger new clothes and a catered dinner.

34. Why does this gesture upset Max?
    A. He thinks that Dalton is only doing it to arouse more sympathy for himself.
    B. He thinks the people who may be chosen for the jury will be influenced by the gesture.
    C. He wants Dalton to recognize that material gestures do not help the oppressed endure the suppression of their human needs.
    D. He was planning to have the communist party make the same gesture, and a is irritated that Dalton beat him to it.

35. How does the presence of Bigger's family and friends make him feel?
    A. He is ashamed because they expose his weaknesses.
    B. He is filled with remorse because he has put them through so much agony.
    C. He realizes how much they really love him, and he is filled with a new sense of peace.
    D. He is relieved to know they are safe.

*Native Son* Multiple Choice Study Questions Page 8

36. What does Bigger think they should feel?
    A. He thinks they should deny that they know him, to save themselves.
    B. He thinks they should be glad, and should be able to feel a part of the freedom and elation he experienced.
    C. He thinks they should be ashamed of themselves for mistreating him for so long that he was driven to commit the crimes.
    D. He thinks they should feel angry at the whites who caused his and their problems.

37. Buckley tries to get Bigger to admit that someone else was involved. Who is it, and why?
    A. He tries to implicate Mr. Dalton, to prove it is all a publicity stunt.
    B. He tries to implicate Bigger's friends and family. He thinks it will help him in his campaign if he can get more Negroes behind bars.
    C. He tries to implicate the employment agency that sent Bigger to Mr. Dalton. He portrays it as a plot by Negroes to kill rich whites.
    D. He tries to implicate Jan. He does not believe a black man could think of and commit such a crime alone, and he wants to implicate the communists.

38. How does Buckley manipulate Bigger?
    A. He offers to support Bigger's family for the next ten years in return for a confession.
    B. He tells Bigger he can get a lighter sentence if he confesses.
    C. He wears Bigger out by saying he knows how bad it feels to be black, accusing him of other crimes, and hinting at sending Bigger to a mental hospital.
    D. He describes the kind of life Mary could have had, and how much good she could have done for the blacks. He makes Bigger feel he has committed the crime against his own people.

39. Why is Bessie's body put on exhibition at the inquest?
    A. The prosecutor wanted to try Bigger for that crime as well.
    B. It was a state law.
    C. The coroner wanted to stir up hatred and get a conviction against Bigger.
    D. The Communist Party insisted on it to show that Bigger's crime was not racially motivated.

40. Where do the police and reporters take Bigger after the inquest? Why?
    A. They take him to the morgue to see the bones, to be sure he realizes what he has done.
    B. They take him to the Dalton residence to reenact the rape and murder, partly for their own amusement and partly because it will sell papers.
    C. They take him to City Hall and put him on display in the lobby. They want to warn other blacks not to imitate his behavior.
    D. They take him to the state mental hospital. They have to prove that he is sane and capable of standing trial.

Native Son Multiple Choice Study Questions Page 9

41. Does Max really understand Bigger's feelings?
    A. Yes, he does. He, too, has felt persecuted as a minority, and fully understands Bigger's innermost feelings.
    B. No, he doesn't. He only sees Bigger as a victim of an oppressive, capitalistic society, and doesn't hear the human needs Bigger is trying to express.

42. How does Bigger feel after the conversation with Max?
    A. He feels even more hopeless because he realizes that since Max is also a member of a hated minority, he has little credibility with the judge and jury.
    B. He feels more relaxed than he has ever felt before, free of much of the strain and stress that has controlled him.
    C. He accepts the responsibility of his actions, and feels resigned to his fate.
    D. He thinks of Max as just another lying white man, and he doesn't trust him.

43. Why does Bigger become fearful after speaking to Max?
    A. He is afraid that if the press associate him with the communists, his family will be harmed.
    B. He doesn't trust Max, and fears that his comments to Max will be used against him in court.
    C. He feels he has made himself vulnerable and yet recognizes to a certain extent that he spoke to Max man-to-man without his usual barriers.
    D. He suddenly questions whether he should be trusting any white man, especially one who is a member of such a radical organization.

44. What had Bigger felt and caught a glimpse of for the first time in his life?
    A. He felt a connection with the rest of humanity.
    B. He felt accountable for his actions.
    C. He felt hatred for blacks as well as whites.
    D. He felt the power of God's forgiveness and love.

45. For what does Max plead?
    A. He pleads for a sentence of insanity so that Bigger can be rehabilitated.
    B. He pleads for the death penalty because Bigger asks for it.
    C. He pleads for a change of venue so that Bigger has more of a chance of getting a fair trial.
    D. He pleads for a life sentence.

46. Does Max ever understand Bigger?
    A. Yes, he does.
    B. No, he doesn't.

# ANSWER KEY - MULTIPLE CHOICE STUDY/QUIZ QUESTIONS
## *Native Son*

| Book One | Book Two | Book Three |
|---|---|---|
| 1. A | 16. D | 30. A |
| 2. C | 17. B | 31. C |
| 3. D | 18. A | 32. B |
| 4. B | 19. B | 33. D |
| 5. C | 20. D | 34. C |
| 6. B | 21. C | 35. A |
| 7. D | 22. B | 36. B |
| 8. A | 23. C | 37. D |
| 9. C | 24. D | 38. C |
| 10. B | 25. A | 39. C |
| 11. B | 26. B | 40. B |
| 12. A | 27. C | 41. B |
| 13. C | 28. D | 42. B |
| 14. A | 29. C | 43. C |
| 15. C |  | 44. A |
|  |  | 45. D |
|  |  | 46. B |

# PREREADING VOCABULARY WORKSHEETS

# VOCABULARY - *Native Son*

<u>Book One: Fear</u>

Part I: Using Prior Knowledge and Contextual Clues

Below are the sentences in which the vocabulary words appear in the text. Read the sentence. Use any clues you can find in the sentence combined with your prior knowledge, and write what you think the underlined words mean on the lines provided.

1. A <u>surly</u> grunt sounded above the tinny ring of metal.

_____

2. "What do I do now?" he demanded <u>belligerently</u>.

_____

3. Bigger went to the window and stood looking out <u>abstractedly</u> into the street.

_____

4. The song <u>irked</u> him and he was glad when she stopped. . . .

_____

5. For a moment they were silent, . . ., their lips compressed to hold down the mounting <u>impulse</u> to laugh.

_____

6. . . . the pigeon rose swiftly through the air on wings stretched so <u>taut</u> and sheer that Bigger could see the gold of the sun through their translucent tips.

_____

7. . . . all but Gus had <u>consented</u>. The way things stood now there were three against Gus . . . .

_____

8. Thy <u>hysterical</u> tensity of his nerves urged him to speak, to free himself.

_____

9. Bigger felt an urgent need to hide his growing and deepening feeling of hysteria; he had to get rid of it or else he would <u>succumb</u> to it.

_____

*Native Son* Vocabulary Book One: Fear - Part I - Page 2

10. And it was his <u>sullen</u> stare and the violent action that followed that made Gus and Jack and G.H. hate and fear him . . . .

___

11. . . . the rich woman and the rich man <u>vowed</u> never to leave each other and to forgive each other.

___

12. He felt <u>impelled</u> to say something to ease the swelling in his chest.

___

13. . . . he passed his days trying to defeat or <u>gratify</u> powerful impulses in a world he feared.

___

14. . . . and he had been sent to the reform school. He felt guilty, <u>condemned</u>.

___

15. At that moment he felt toward Mary and Jan a dumb, cold, and <u>inarticulate</u> hate.

___

16. . . . it seemed that the pressure of Jan's fingers had left an <u>indelible</u> imprint.

___

17. He stepped backward, as though she were contaminated with an invisible <u>contagion</u>.

___

18. <u>Apprehensively</u>, he looked up at the big house. It was dark and silent.

___

19. As he took his hands from the pillow he heard a long slow sigh . . ., a sigh which afterwards, when he remembered it, seemed final, <u>irrevocable</u>.

___

20. Gradually, the intensity of his sensations <u>subsided</u>, and he was aware of the room.

___

*Native Son* Vocabulary Book One: Fear Part II

Part II: Determining the Meaning
You have tried to figure out the meanings of the vocabulary words for Book One: Fear. Now match the vocabulary words to their dictionary definitions. If there are words for which you cannot figure out the definition by contextual clues and by process of elimination, look them up in a dictionary.

___ 1. surly                A. tense; tight

___ 2. belligerently        B. give in; come under the influence of

___ 3. abstractedly         C. having uncontrolled emotions

___ 4. irked                D. promised

___ 5. impulse              E. motivated; had the feeling of needing to do something

___ 6. taut                 F. found guilt or unfit

___ 7. consented            G. sulky

___ 8. hysterical           H. In a manner apart from the situation

___ 9. succumb              I. hostilely

___ 10. sullen              J. agreed

___ 11. vowed               K. irritated; bothered

___ 12. impelled            L. permanent

___ 13. gratify             M. easily transmitted disease

___ 14. condemned           N. bad-humored; gruff

___ 15. inarticulate        O. quieted; settled

___ 16. indelible           P. inclination; motivating force

___ 17. contagion           Q. satisfy; indulge

___ 18. apprehensively      R. can't be taken back or sent back

___ 19. irrevocable         S. anxiously; fearfully

___ 20. subsided            T. wordless; speechless

Vocabulary - *Native Son* Book Two: Flight

Part I: Using Prior Knowledge and Contextual Clues

    Below are the sentences in which the vocabulary words appear in the text. Read the sentence. Use any clues you can find in the sentence combined with your prior knowledge, and write what you think the underlined words mean on the lines provided.

1. Then, in answer to a <u>foreboding</u> call from a dark part of his mind, he leaped from bed . . . .

_____

2. Then fear <u>rendered</u> his legs like water.

_____

3. Why couldn't she wait until he told her of his own <u>accord</u>?

_____

4. . . . he felt that he was arriving at something which had long <u>eluded</u> him.

_____

5. . . . he had to get that <u>lingering</u> image of Mary's bloody head lying on those newspapers from before his eyes.

_____

6. . . . that there should be a way in which gnawing hunger and restless <u>aspiration</u> could be fused.

_____

7. . . . for in actions such as these he felt that there was a way to escape from this tight <u>morass</u> of fear and shame . . . .

_____

8. . . . his hope toward a vague and <u>benevolent</u> something that would help and lead him . . . .

_____

9. One of them <u>anarchists</u> who's agin the government.

_____

10. He seemed sort of <u>peeved</u> when I told him she was gone.

_____

*Native Son* Vocabulary Book Two: Flight - Part I - Page 2

11. . . . he had long been <u>yearning</u> for weapons to hold in his hands . . .

___

12. When he took his lips away he looked at her with eyes full of <u>reproach</u> . . . .

___

13. Here's to you, even if you don't want to talk and even if you is acting <u>queer</u>.

___

14. The warm room <u>lulled</u> his blood and a deepening sense of fatigue drugged him with sleep.

___

15. He imagined that if he shook it he would see pieces of bone falling into the bin and he knew that he would not be able to <u>endure</u> it.

___

16. Yet he knew of no way to <u>atone</u> for his guilt . . . .

___

17. Strength <u>ebbed</u> from him.

___

18. Bigger hesitated. He suspected a trap. But if Jan really had an <u>alibi</u>, then he had to talk; he had to steer them away from himself.

___

19. It was <u>conjectured</u> that perhaps the family had information to the effect that Erlone knew of the whereabouts of Miss Dalton, and certain police officials assigned that as the motive . . . .

___

20. He had to now. <u>Imperiously</u> driven, he rode roughshod over her whimpering protests, feeling acutely sorry for her as he galloped a frenzied horse down a steep hill in the face of a resisting wind. . . .

___

*Native Son* Vocabulary Book Two: Flight - Part I - Page 3

21. . . . her bloody mouth open in <u>awe</u> and wonder and pain and accusation?

_____

22. . . . over and above all that had happened, <u>impalpable</u> but real, there remained to him a queer sense of power.

_____

23. . . . the world seemed to him a strange <u>labyrinth</u> even when the streets were straight and the walls were square . . . .

_____

24. Immediately a cordon of five thousand police, <u>augmented</u> by more than three thousand volunteers . . . .

_____

25. Police and <u>vigilantes</u>, armed with rifles . . . began at 18th Street this morning and are searching every Negro home . . . .

_____

26. In a radio broadcast last night, Mayor Ditz warned of possible mob violence and <u>exhorted</u> the public to maintain order.

_____

*Native Son* Vocabulary Book Two: Flight Part II

Part II: Determining the Meaning
You have tried to figure out the meanings of the vocabulary words for Book Two: Flight. Now match the vocabulary words to their dictionary definitions. If there are words for which you cannot figure out the definition by contextual clues and by process of elimination, look them up in a dictionary.

___ 21. foreboding
___ 22. rendered
___ 23. accord
___ 24. eluded
___ 25. lingering
___ 26. aspiration
___ 27. morass
___ 28. benevolent
___ 29. anarchists
___ 30. peeved
___ 31. yearning
___ 32. reproach
___ 33. queer
___ 34. lulled
___ 35. endure
___ 36. ebbed
___ 37. alibi
___ 38. conjectured
___ 39. imperiously
___ 40. awe
___ 41. impalpable
___ 42. labyrinth
___ 43. augmented
___ 44. vigilantes
___ 45. exhorted

A. ambition
B. suggestive of doing good
C. escaped from one's understanding
D. agreement
E. one who is against all forms of government
F. predicting something bad for the future
G. something that hinders, engulfs, or overwhelms
H. maze
I. remaining, as though reluctant to leave
J. carry on through hardships
K. added to; supplemented
L. to flow from
M. calmed
N. strange
O. vexed; angry
P. disapproval
Q. thought; came to a conclusion based on present evidence
R. an excuse; a way to prove one could not have committed a crime
S. longing
T. a mixed emotion of reverence, respect and dread
U. can't be grasped by touch or in the mind
V. made; caused to be
W. overbearingly; pressingly, urgently
X. people who take the law into their own hands
Y. urged through arguments and appeals

Vocabulary - *Native Son* Book Three: Fate

Part I: Using Prior Knowledge and Contextual Clues

    Below are the sentences in which the vocabulary words appear in the text. Read the sentence. Use any clues you can find in the sentence combined with your prior knowledge, and write what you think the underlined words mean on the lines provided.

1. . . . so why not reach inward and kill that which had <u>duped</u> him?

_____

2. . . . he looked without hope or resentment, his eyes like two still pools of black ink in his <u>flaccid</u> face.

_____

3. Maybe the confused promptings, the excitement, the tingling, the <u>elation</u>--maybe they were false lights that led nowhere.

_____

4. . . . images which in turn aroused impulses long <u>dormant</u>, impulses that he had suppressed and sought to shunt from his life.

_____

5. . . . he knew that they were <u>futile</u>, that the people who stood along the wall back of him had the destiny of him and his family in their hands.

_____

6. "He didn't have nothing to do with it," said Bigger, feeling a keen desire on the man's part to have him <u>implicate</u> Jan.

_____

7. He lay on the cold floor sobbing; but really he was standing up strongly with <u>contrite</u> heart, holding his life in his hands, staring at it with a wondering question.

_____

8. Mr. Max, we are allowing plenty of <u>latitude</u> here.

_____

9. Well, to charge them less rent would be <u>unethical</u>.

_____

*Native Son* Vocabulary Book Three: Fate - Part I - Page 2

10. They were using his having killed Bessie to kill him for his having killed Mary, to cast him in a light that would <u>sanction</u> any action taken to destroy him.

_____

11. We'll enter a plea of not guilty at the <u>arraignment</u> tomorrow.

_____

12. But so far only the certainty of death was his; only the <u>unabating</u> hate of the white faces could be seen. . . .

_____

13. I want to prevail upon this Court to consider this boy's plea of guilty as evidence <u>mitigating</u> his punishment.

_____

14. A change of <u>venue</u> is of no value now.

_____

15. . . . every man and woman in this nation can stand and view how <u>inextricably</u> our hopes and fears of today create the exultation and doom of tomorrow.

_____

16. Who, then, fanned this <u>latent</u> hate into fury?

_____

17. . . . where did he get such a vision as to make him, without <u>premeditation</u> snatch the life of another person so quickly and instinctively . . . .

_____

18. . . . Negroes . . . are struggling within unbelievably narrow limits to achieve that feeling of at-home-ness for which we once strove so <u>ardently</u>.

_____

19. He did not stir; he lay still, feeling that by being still he would <u>stave</u> off feeling and thinking

_____

20. . . . and though he <u>imputed</u> to Max the feelings he wanted to grasp, he could not talk of them to Max until he had forgotten Max's presence.

_____

*Native Son* Vocabulary Book Three: Fate Part II

Part II: Determining the Meaning

You have tried to figure out the meanings of the vocabulary words for Book Three: Fate. Now match the vocabulary words to their dictionary definitions. If there are words for which you cannot figure out the definition by contextual clues and by process of elimination, look them up in a dictionary.

___ 46. duped

___ 47. flaccid

___ 48. elation

___ 49. dormant

___ 50. futile

___ 51. implicate

___ 52. contrite

___ 53. latitude

___ 54. unethical

___ 55. sanction

___ 56. arraignment

___ 57. unabating

___ 58. mitigating

___ 59. venue

___ 60. inextricably

___ 61. latent

___ 62. ardently

___ 63. stave

___ 64. imputed

A. leeway; freedom within regulations

B. feeling of extreme happiness or pleasure

C. lacking firmness or muscle tone

D. location (city, state) where a trial is held

E. to call an accused person to court to answer the charges against him/her

F. put off; postpone

G. dormant; present but not evident or active

H. deceived; made foolish

I. wrong; not within accept guidelines

J. approve

K. useless

L. enthusiastically; fervently

M. attributed; credited

N. asleep inactive

O. condition of not being able to escape from

P. sorry for past actions

Q. not subsiding; not becoming less

R. connect incriminatingly

S. making more moderate

# ANSWER KEY - VOCABULARY
*Native Son*

<u>Book One: Fear</u>
1. N
2. I
3. H
4. K
5. P
6. A
7. J
8. C
9. B
10. G
11. D
12. E
13. Q
14. F
15. T
16. L
17. M
18. S
19. R
20. O

<u>Book Two: Flight</u>
21. F
22. V
23. D
24. C
25. I
26. A
27. G
28. B
29. E
30. O
31. S
32. P
33. N
34. M
35. J
36. L
37. R
38. Q
39. W
40. T
41. U
42. H
43. K
44. X
45. Y

<u>Book Three: Fate</u>
46. H
47. C
48. B
49. N
50. K
51. R
52. P
53. A
54. I
55. J
56. E
57. Q
58. S
59. D
60. O
61. G
62. L
63. F
64. M

# DAILY LESSONS

# LESSON ONE

Objectives
    1. To introduce the *Native Son* unit.
    2. To distribute books and other related materials
    3. To preview the study questions for Book One
    4. To familiarize students with the vocabulary for Book One

NOTE: This introduction requires that you have put up a bulletin board as follows:
    Title the board NATIVE SON. Under the title, divide the board into three sections and title each: FEAR, FLIGHT and FATE. In the FEAR section, place pictures of things which cause fear or people who look afraid. In the FLIGHT section, place pictures of things in flight or fleeing (airplane, bird, person running away, etc.). In the FATE section, place pictures of things that represent different fates of people (person in jail, person winning the lottery, poor person, rich person, etc.).

Activity #1
    Ask students to look at the bulletin board. (If you do not have a bulletin board, you can tape the pictures noted above onto bulletin board paper on the chalk board or on a wall.) Explain that the book students are about to read is divided into three sections titled FEAR, FLIGHT, and FATE. Explain that the meanings of these three words as titles for the sections of the book are significant.
    Point out the examples of FEAR. Ask students what things in their lives make them fearful.
    Ask students to define FLIGHT. What kinds of flight are there? Does FLIGHT imply freedom (as the symbolic bird flying) or can it imply other things, too? What kinds of things can it imply?
    Ask students to define FATE. What is fate? Who, if anyone or anything, controls our fates? Do we have any control over our own destinies?

Activity #2
    Distribute the materials students will use in this unit. Explain in detail how students are to use these materials.

    Study Guides  Students should read the study guide questions for each reading assignment prior to beginning the reading assignment to get a feeling for what events and ideas are important in the section they are about to read. After reading the section, students will (as a class or individually) answer the questions to review the important events and ideas from that section of the book. Students should keep the study guides as study materials for the unit test.

    Vocabulary  Prior to reading a reading assignment, students will do vocabulary work related to the section of the book they are about to read. Following the completion of the reading of the book, there will be a vocabulary review of all the words used in the vocabulary assignments. Students should keep their vocabulary work as study materials for the unit test.

    Reading Assignment Sheet   You need to fill in the reading assignment sheet to let students know by when their reading has to be completed. You can either write the assignment sheet up on a side blackboard or bulletinb oard and leave it there for students to see each day, or you can "ditto" copies for each student to have. In either case, you should advise students to become very familiar with the reading assignments so they know what is expected of them.

    Extra Activities Center   The Extra Activities page in this unit contains suggestions for an extra library of related books and articles in your classroom as well as crossword and word search puzzles.  Make an extra activities center in your room where you will keep these materials for students to use. (Bring the books and articles in from the library and keep several copies of the puzzles on hand.) Explain to students that these materials are available for students to use when they finish reading assignments or other class work early.

    Nonfiction Assignment Sheet   Explain to students that they each are to read at least one non-fiction piece from the in-class library at some time during the unit. Students will fill out a nonfiction assignment sheet after completing the reading to help you evaluate their reading experiences and to help the students think about and evaluate their own reading experiences.

    Books   Each school has its own rules and regulations regarding student use of school books. Advise students of the procedures that are normal for your school.

## Activity #3
    Preview the study questions and have students do the vocabulary work for Book One of *Native Son*. If students do not finish this assignment during this class period, they should complete it prior to the next class meeting.

# NONFICTION ASSIGNMENT SHEET
(To be completed after reading the required nonfiction article)

Name _____ Date _____

Title of Nonfiction Read _____

Written By _____ Publication Date _____

I. Factual Summary: Write a short summary of the piece you read.



II. Vocabulary
    1. With which vocabulary words in the piece did you encounter some degree of difficulty?


    2. How did you resolve your lack of understanding with these words?


III. Interpretation: What was the main point the author wanted you to get from reading his work?


IV. Criticism
    1. With which points of the piece did you agree or find easy to accept? Why?


    2. With which points of the piece did you disagree or find difficult to believe? Why?


V. Personal Response: What do you think about this piece? <u>OR</u> How does this piece influence your ideas?

## LESSON TWO

Objectives
1. To preview the study questions for Book One of *Native Son*
2. To preview the vocabulary for Book One
3. To read Book One
4. To give students the opportunity to practice oral reading
5. To give the teacher the opportunity to evaluate students' reading skills

Activity #1
    Give students about twenty minutes to preview the study questions and to do the related vocabulary work for Book One of *Native Son*.

Activity #2
    Have students read Book One of *Native Son* out loud in class. You probably know the best way to get readers with your class; pick students at random, ask for volunteers, or use whatever method works best for your group. If you have not yet completed an oral reading evaluation for your students this marking period, this would be a good opportunity to do so. A form is included with this unit for your convenience.
    Tell students that they should complete reading Book One prior to Lesson Four. (Give students a day/date.)


## LESSON THREE

Objectives
1. To introduce the project associated with this unit
2. To give students practice using the library's resources
3. To make students more educated about our world
4. To show students various viewpoints about issues related to *Native Son*


Activity
    Distribute the Project Assignment Sheet. Discuss the directions in detail and give students the remainder of this class period to begin working on their projects.

Teacher Note: On the Project Assignment Sheet we have used the term "Black Americans" instead of the more recently correct "Afro-Americans" intentionally -- not to offend anyone, but because there are many people of dark skin in America who face many of the same issues as Afro-Americans. We were simply searching for a more general term of classification.

# PROJECT ASSIGNMENT SHEET - *Native Son*

## PROMPT

In his book *Native Son*, Richard Wright touches on many complex issues in our society. The central focus of the book is on the plight of the black man; that is, the inherent problems a black person had/has in our society. Another central theme in the novel is the idea of seeing a person as *a person* rather than a *black* person or a *white* person. Ideally, with prejudice totally out of the picture, a person would be seen as neither black nor white -- just a person without skin color entering into our consciousness at all. How we face and attempt to overcome racial prejudice is another important theme in *Native Son*. Other ideas touched upon in *Native Son* include the influence of Communism and the functioning of our criminal justice system relating to racial issues. *Native Son* is, too, among other things, a stunning, graphic, psychological portrait of one black man's life.

This novel presents us with several important ideas, each of which we could delve into in detail and spend months researching, discussing, and debating. One thing that is important to recognize is that this book was written in 1940. In addition to delving into the issues that faced the main character of this novel, we need to "bring the book to date" and evaluate the racial issues that face Americans today. Notice that I did not specify issues that face *black* Americans or *white* Americans. Racial issues affect everyone in the country. They are deep-rooted and widespread, and affect many aspects of our daily lives, whether we all realize that or not.

## ASSIGNMENT

Your assignment is to read at least five nonfiction articles relating in some way to racial issues in America. You may choose from the Suggested Topics list below, or you may research some other relevant aspect that particularly interests you. The whole point of this assignment is to help make you more aware of different viewpoints, historical aspects, current ideas, what has been done, what is being done, and what may be done relating to racial issues in America as well as to make you more familiar with other issues that were brought up in the book *Native Son*.

As you read your articles, take notes. You will need to use your notes later to make a presentation to the class and to complete a writing assignment. In addition, fill out one of the Nonfiction Assignment Sheets for each article you read.

## SUGGESTED TOPICS

- Communism in America
- The American Criminal Justice System
- The Civil Rights Movement
- Political Influences of Black Americans
- Issues Facing Black Americans Today
- Economic Issues Relating to Black Americans
- Education Issues Relating to Black Americans
- Anti-Discrimination Laws
- Quotas
- Equal Opportunity Laws
- Issues Facing Urban Black Americans
- Issues Facing Rural Black Americans
- The Welfare System as a Help or a Hindrance to Black Americans

This is just a little list with a few general suggestions to get you thinking. There are probably several hundred specific topics that would be appropriate for this assignment.

# LESSON FOUR

Objectives
    1. To review the main events and ideas from Book One
    2. To preview the study questions for Book Two
    3. To familiarize students with the vocabulary in Book Two
    4. To read Book Two

Activity #1
    Give students a few minutes to formulate answers for the study guide questions for Book One, and then discuss the answers to the questions in detail. Write the answers on the board or overhead transparency so students can have the correct answers for study purposes. Note: It is a good practice in public speaking and leadership skills for individual students to take charge of leading the discussions of the study questions. Perhaps a different student could go to the front of the class and lead the discussion each day that the study questions are discussed during this unit. Of course, the teacher should guide the discussion when appropriate and be sure to fill in any gaps the students leave.

Activity #2
    Give students about twenty minutes to preview the study questions for Book Two of *Native Son* and to do the related vocabulary work.

Activity #3
    Have students read Book Two of *Native Son* out loud in class. You probably know the best way to get readers with your class; pick students at random, ask for volunteers, or use whatever method works best for your group. If you have not yet completed an oral reading evaluation for your students this marking period, this would be a good opportunity to do so. A form is included with this unit for your convenience.
    Tell students that they should complete reading Book Two prior to Lesson Seven (give students a day/date).


# LESSON FIVE

Objective
    To read Book Two of *Native Son*

Activity
    Give students this class period to work on the reading assignment. If you need to finish the oral reading evaluations, have students read orally. Otherwise, have students read silently during this class period.

# ORAL READING EVALUATION - *Native Son*

Name _____ Class_____ Date _____

| SKILL | EXCELLENT | GOOD | AVERAGE | FAIR | POOR |
|---|---|---|---|---|---|
| Fluency | 5 | 4 | 3 | 2 | 1 |
| Clarity | 5 | 4 | 3 | 2 | 1 |
| Audibility | 5 | 4 | 3 | 2 | 1 |
| Pronunciation | 5 | 4 | 3 | 2 | 1 |
| _____ | 5 | 4 | 3 | 2 | 1 |
| _____ | 5 | 4 | 3 | 2 | 1 |

Total _____ Grade _____

Comments:

# LESSON SIX

Objectives

    1. To give students the opportunity to think about one of the central themes of the novel: fear
    2. To give students the opportunity to practice writing to inform
    3. To give the teacher the opportunity to evaluate students' writing skills

Activity

    Distribute Writing Assignment #1. Discuss the directions in detail and give students ample time to complete the assignment.

# LESSONS SEVEN AND EIGHT

Objectives

    1. To check to see that students read Book Two as assigned
    2. To review the main ideas and events from Book Two
    3. To preview the study questions for Book Three
    4. To familiarize students with the vocabulary in Book Three
    5. To read Book Three
    6. To evaluate students' oral reading

Activity #1

    Quiz - Distribute quizzes and give students about 10 minutes to complete them. (Note: The quizzes may either be the short answer study guides or the multiple choice version for Book Two.) Have students exchange papers. Grade the quizzes as a class. Collect the papers for recording the grades. (If you used the multiple choice version as a quiz, take a few minutes to discuss the answers for the short answer version if your students are using the short answer version for their study guides.)

Activity #2

    Give students about 20 minutes to preview the study questions and to do the related vocabulary work for Book Three.

Activity #3

    Tell students that prior to Lesson Nine they must complete reading Book Three of *Native Son*. They will have the remainder of this class period (Lesson Seven) and all of the next class period (Lesson Eight) to work on this assignment.

# WRITING ASSIGNMENT #1 - *Native Son*

## PROMPT

The title of the first book of *Native Son* is "Fear." Your assignment is to write a composition in which you explain why the title "Fear" is appropriate for the first section of this book.

## PREWRITING

In your mind (and with your text if necessary) review all the possible meanings of the word "fear" in Book One. Jot them down on a piece of paper. Include any appropriate examples from the text to illustrate your ideas.

Look at your notes. Try to find a way to make one statement which will include all of your ideas, all the facets of "fear" in this section of the novel. That one statement will become your thesis, your main idea for your composition.

## DRAFTING

Write a paragraph in which you introduce your thesis, your main idea.

Write one paragraph for each of the different facets of "fear" in Book One. In each paragraph use a topic sentence to state your idea and then use examples from the text to support your statement.

Write a paragraph in which you bring together all of your ideas and make your conclusions and concluding remarks.

## PROMPT

When you finish the rough draft of your paper, ask a student who sits near you to read it. After reading your rough draft, he/she should tell you what he/she liked best about your work, which parts were difficult to understand, and ways in which your work could be improved. Reread your paper considering your critic's comments, and make the corrections you think are necessary.

## PROOFREADING

Do a final proofreading of your paper double-checking your grammar, spelling, organization, and the clarity of your ideas.

# LESSON NINE

Objectives
1. To review the main ideas and events from Book Three
2. To discuss *Native Son* on interpretive and critical levels

Activity #1
Give students a few minutes to formulate answers to the study questions for Book Three. Discuss the answers and have students jot down the "correct" answers for study use.

Activity #2
Choose the questions from the Extra Discussion Questions/Writing Assignments which seem most appropriate for your students. A class discussion of these questions is most effective if students have been given the opportunity to formulate answers to the questions prior to the discussion. To this end, you may either have all the students formulate answers to all the questions, divide your class into groups and assign one or more questions to each group, or you could assign one question to each student in your class. The option you choose will make a difference in the amount of class time needed for this activity.

After students have had ample time to formulate answers to the questions, begin your class discussion of the questions and the ideas presented by the questions. Be sure students take notes during the discussion so they have information to study for the unit test.

# EXTRA WRITING ASSIGNMENTS/DISCUSSION QUESTIONS - *Native Son*

<u>Interpretation</u>

1. From what point of view is *Native Son* written, and what effect does that have on the story?

2. Is the story of *Native Son* believable? Explain why or why not.

3. Where is the climax of the story? Explain your choice.

4. Are the characters in *Native Son* stereotypes? If so, explain the usefulness of employing stereotypes in the novel. If they are not, explain how they merit individuality.

5. What is the setting of the story? Could this story have been set in a different time and place and still have the same effect?

6. What are the main conflicts in the story? Are they resolved? How or why not?

<u>Critical</u>

7. Explain the significance of the title of *Native Son*.

8. Are Bigger's actions believably motivated? Explain why or why not.

9. Characterize Richard Wright's style of writing. How does it contribute to the value of the novel?

10. Describe Bigger's relationship with his family.

11. Compare and contrast Mr. Dalton and Jan.

12. Describe Bigger's relationship with Bessie.

13. Describe Bigger's relationship to Gus.

14. What is Bessie's role in *Native Son*? What does she add to the story, and how would the story have been different without her?

15. Who was responsible for Mary's death? Explain your choice.

16. Describe Jan's attitude towards Bigger.

17. Is Mr. Dalton a hypocrite? If so, explain how. If not, explain why not.

*Native Son* Extra Discussion Questions page 2

18. Were Mary, Jan and Max actually cruel to Bigger? If so, how? If not, why not?

19. How would the essence of the novel have changed if Bigger had been granted a life sentence?

20. Give examples of the major symbols in the novel and explain the use and meaning of each.

21. Explain the significance of Bigger's name.

21. Why did Bigger always want to read accounts of his crimes and trial in the newspaper?

22. What is the role of education in the story?

23. What is the role of religion in the story?

24. How does Bigger deal with his own feelings of fear?

25. Why does Bigger have to cut off Mary's head? Why doesn't Richard Wright have her fit neatly into the furnace?

26. Discuss Bigger's character development throughout the novel.

<u>Personal Response</u>

27. Did you enjoy reading *Native Son*? Why or why not?

28. One of the main themes of the book is "fear." What things do we have to fear in our society today?

29. Define the word "fate."

30. Many books (both fact and fiction) have been written about the lives of black people in America in the last century. Compare and contrast *Native Son* with another such book you have read.

## LESSON TEN

Objective
    To review all of the vocabulary work done in this unit

Activity
    Choose one (or more) of the vocabulary review activities listed below and spend your class period as directed in the activity. Some of the materials for these review activities are located in the Vocabulary Resource section of this unit.

### VOCABULARY REVIEW ACTIVITIES

1. Divide your class into two teams and have an old-fashioned spelling or definition bee.

2. Give each of your students (or students in groups of two, three or four) a *Native Son* Vocabulary Word Search Puzzle. The person (group) to find all of the vocabulary words in the puzzle first wins.

3. Give students a *Native Son* Vocabulary Word Search Puzzle without the word list. The person or group to find the most vocabulary words in the puzzle wins.

4. Use a *Native Son* Vocabulary Crossword Puzzle. Put the puzzle onto a transparency on the overhead projector (so everyone can see it), and do the puzzle together as a class.

5. Give students a *Native Son* Vocabulary Matching Worksheet to do.

6. Divide your class into two teams. Use the *Native Son* vocabulary words with their letters jumbled as a word list. Student 1 from Team A faces off against Student 1 from Team B. You write the first jumbled word on the board. The first student (1A or 1B) to unscramble the word wins the chance for his/her team to score points. If 1A wins the jumble, go to student 2A and give him/her a definition. He/she must give you the correct spelling of the vocabulary word which fits that definition. If he/she does, Team A scores a point, and you give student 3A a definition for which you expect a correctly spelled matching vocabulary word. Continue giving Team A definitions until some team member makes an incorrect response. An incorrect response sends the game back to the jumbled-word face off, this time with students 2A and 2B. Instead of repeating giving definitions to the first few students of each team, continue with the student after the one who gave the last incorrect response on the team. For example, if Team B wins the jumbled-word face-off, and student 5B gave the last incorrect answer for Team B, you would start this round of definition questions with student 6B, and so on. The team with the most points wins!

7. Have students write a story in which they correctly use as many vocabulary words as possible. Have students read their compositions orally! Post the most original compositions on your bulletin board!

# LESSONS ELEVEN AND TWELVE

Objectives
    1. To study the symbols, images and themes in *Native Son*
    2. To give students the opportunity to work together in small groups
    3. To help students review the text and find important ideas they may have missed on the first reading
    4. To gather basic information which will be used in a discussion of the themes of the novel

Activity #1
    Divide your class into groups--one group for each of the following topics:
        1. Sleep/Awake (and Dream/Reality)
        2. Time
        3. Light/Dark
        4. Death/Murder
        5. Violence
        6. Heat/Cold
        7. Blindness

Each group should look at its topic through the entire novel. Group members should divide the work into books, giving each person of the group a specific book to research. Each member should find all the references made to the group's topic within his/her section of the book. After each member has had time to complete his/her research, the group members should share their findings with each other. They should have a small group discussion to try to draw any reasonable conclusions they can from the data they collected. One group member should be designated "secretary" to jot down the group's ideas from the discussion. Another member should be designated "spokesperson" to report the group's ideas to the class.

Activity #2
    The groups will each report their findings and conclusions to the whole class. The teacher or a student should write down on the board or overhead all of the findings and conclusions. Students should take notes for study use. Use the group reports as springboards for discussions of each of the topics assigned.

# LESSON THIRTEEN

Objectives
1. To give students the opportunity to express their own opinions in writing
2. To help students review their nonfiction reading and prepare for the oral presentation
3. To give the teacher the opportunity to evaluate students' writing skills

Activity

Distribute Writing Assignment #2. Discuss the directions in detail and give students ample time to complete the assignment.

# LESSONS FOURTEEN AND FIFTEEN

Objectives
1. To widen the breadth of students' knowledge about the topics discussed or touched upon in *Native Son*
2. To check students' nonfiction reading assignments

Activity

Ask each student to give a brief oral report about the nonfiction articles he/she read for the unit project assignment. Your criteria for evaluating this report will vary depending on the level of your students. You may wish for students to give a complete report without using notes of any kind, or you may want students to read directly from a written report, or you may want to do something in between these two extremes. Just make students aware of your criteria in ample time for them to prepare their reports.

Start with one student's report. After that, ask if anyone else in the class has read on a topic related to the first student's report. If no one has, choose another student at random. After each report, be sure to ask if anyone has a report related to the one just completed. That will help keep a continuity during the discussion of the reports. After all reports on a topic are given, take a minute to hold a short class discussion about the information students have just heard.

# WRITING ASSIGNMENT #2 - *Native Son*

## PROMPT
By now you should have completed the reading of nonfiction articles for your project assignment. Soon you will have to give an oral report telling about the articles you read. In preparation for that report, your assignment is to review the articles you have read and to write a composition in which you give your own opinions about the topic you have researched.

## PREWRITING
Most of your prewriting has been done already since you took notes while you read and filled out a Nonfiction Assignment Sheet for each of the articles you read. Take time now to review all of your notes and to think about the topic you have chosen. Write one sentence that states your own view(s) about the topic you have chosen. Next to that sentence, jot down at least three reasons why you have adopted this (these) view(s). Next to each reason, jot down examples or ideas that support or illustrate your point.

## DRAFTING
Write a paragraph in which you introduce your topic and state your own viewpoint.
Write one paragraph for each of your reasons for choosing the viewpoint you have. Each paragraph should have a topic sentence stating the reason and should be filled out with examples or ideas that support or illustrate your point.
Write one paragraph in which you make your concluding remarks and bring your composition to a close.

## PROMPT
When you finish the rough draft of your paper, ask a student who sits near you to read it. After reading your rough draft, he/she should tell you what he/she liked best about your work, which parts were difficult to understand, and ways in which your work could be improved. Reread your paper considering your critic's comments, and make the corrections you think are necessary.

## PROOFREADING
Do a final proofreading of your paper double-checking your grammar, spelling, organization, and the clarity of your ideas.

# LESSON SIXTEEN

Objectives
1. To give students the opportunity to practice writing to persuade
2. To help students review the ideas in the book
3. To give the teacher the opportunity to evaluate students' writing skills

Activity #1

Distribute Writing Assignment #3. Discuss the directions in detail and give students ample time to complete the assignment.

While students are working on Writing Assignment #3, call individual students to your desk or some other private area for a writing conference in which you discuss their individual writing skills based on the first two writing assignments in this unit. A writing evaluation form is included with this unit for your convenience.

NOTE: If you are backed up on paper grading and are short on time, you may want to delete this lesson and use Writing Assignment #3 as the essay question for the Unit Test.


# LESSON SEVENTEEN

Objective

To review the main ideas presented in *Native Son*

Activity #1

Choose one of the review games/activities included in the packet and spend your class period as outlined there. Some materials for these activities are located in the Extra Activities Packet section of this unit.

Activity #2

Remind students that the Unit Test will be in the next class meeting. Stress the review of the Study Guides and their class notes as a last minute, brush-up review for homework.

# WRITING ASSIGNMENT #3 - *Native Son*

## PROMPT

One of the first things that one notices upon studying our criminal justice system is that there is a difference between "justice" and "law." One of our rights as citizens of the United States is the right to a fair trial under the law. Certain procedures have been developed to insure that one gets a fair trial. You have probably heard of someone "getting off on a technicality," which means usually that some legal procedure was not followed correctly and therefore the case against the defendant was dismissed (whether he/she was guilty or not). If you are the defendant, you celebrate. If you are the victim, you may be angry or astonished that "justice" was not served. The person who did this thing to you just waltzed out of the courtroom without punishment. Thus, you can see the difference between "justice" and "law."

Your assignment is to write a composition in which you persuade me that justice was (or was not) served in Bigger's case.

## PREWRITING

Review the passages in the text relating to Bigger's trial; specifically the statements made to the court by the two attorneys. Take two pieces of scratch paper. Label one Defense and the other Prosecution. On the Defense paper, jot down the arguments Bigger's attorney made on his behalf. On the Prosecution paper, jot down the arguments the state's attorney made against Bigger. Consider the arguments on both sides. Decide whether or not the sentence the judge gave Bigger was "just" or not. Jot down three reasons why you think the sentence was (or was not) just. Next to each reason jot down some examples, ideas or explanations to support your reason.

## DRAFTING

Write a paragraph in which you introduce the idea that the sentence handed down to Bigger from the judge was (or was not) just.

Write one paragraph for each of the reasons you listed for your decision. Each paragraph should have a topic sentence stating your reason and should be filled out with examples, ideas or explanations to support your reasons.

Write one paragraph in which you draw your conclusions and bring your composition to a close.

## PROMPT

When you finish the rough draft of your paper, ask a student who sits near you to read it. After reading your rough draft, he/she should tell you what he/she liked best about your work, which parts were difficult to understand, and ways in which your work could be improved. Reread your paper considering your critic's comments, and make the corrections you think are necessary.

## PROOFREADING

Do a final proofreading of your paper double-checking your grammar, spelling, organization, and the clarity of your ideas.

# WRITING EVALUATION FORM - *Native Son*

Name _____ Date _____

    Grade _____

Circle One For Each Item:

Grammar:        correct        errors noted on paper

Spelling:         correct        errors noted on paper

Punctuation:     correct        errors noted on paper

Legibility:        excellent    good   fair   poor


Strengths:




Weaknesses:




Comments/Suggestions:

# REVIEW GAMES/ACTIVITIES - *Native Son*

1. Ask the class to make up a unit test for *Native Son*. The test should have 4 sections: matching, true/false, short answer, and essay. Students may use 1/2 period to make the test and then swap papers and use the other 1/2 class period to take a test a classmate has devised. (open book) You may want to use the unit test included in this packet or take questions from the students' unit tests to formulate your own test.

2. Take 1/2 period for students to make up true and false questions (including the answers). Collect the papers and divide the class into two teams. Draw a big tic-tac-toe board on the chalk board. Make one team X and one team O. Ask questions to each side, giving each student one turn. If the question is answered correctly, that students' team's letter (X or O) is placed in the box. If the answer is incorrect, no mark is placed in the box. The object is to get three marks in a row like tic-tac-toe. You may want to keep track of the number of games won for each team.

3. Take 1/2 period for students to make up questions (true/false and short answer). Collect the questions. Divide the class into two teams. You'll alternate asking questions to individual members of teams A & B (like in a spelling bee). The question keeps going from A to B until it is correctly answered, then a new question is asked. A correct answer does not allow the team to get another question. Correct answers are +2 points; incorrect answers are -1 point.

4. Have students pair up and quiz each other from their study guides and class notes.

5. Give students a *Native Son* crossword puzzle to complete.

6. Divide your class into two teams. Use the *Native Son* crossword words with their letters jumbled as a word list. Student 1 from Team A faces off against Student 1 from Team B. You write the first jumbled word on the board. The first student (1A or 1B) to unscramble the word wins the chance for his/her team to score points. If 1A wins the jumble, go to student 2A and give him/her a clue. He/she must give you the correct word which matches that clue. If he/she does, Team A scores a point, and you give student 3A a clue for which you expect another correct response. Continue giving Team A clues until some team member makes an incorrect response. An incorrect response sends the game back to the jumbled-word face off, this time with students 2A and 2B. Instead of repeating giving clues to the first few students of each team, continue with the student after the one who gave the last incorrect response on the team. For example, if Team B wins the jumbled-word face-off, and student 5B gave the last incorrect answer for Team B, you would start this round of clue questions with student 6B, and so on. The team with the most points wins!

# UNIT TESTS

# SHORT ANSWER UNIT TEST 1 - *Native Son*

I. Matching/Identify

\_\_ 1. Peggy         A. Bigger's lawyer

\_\_ 2. Vera          B. Investigator

\_\_ 3. Bigger        C. Bigger's brother

\_\_ 4. Jan           D. Housekeeper

\_\_ 5. Bessie        E. Bigger's girlfriend

\_\_ 6. Mary          F. Rich white girl

\_\_ 7. Max           G. Owns poolroom

\_\_ 8. Gus           H. State prosecutor

\_\_ 9. Buckley       I. Bigger's sister

\_\_ 10. Mrs. Dalton  J. Murders twice

\_\_ 11. Buddy        K. Blind woman

\_\_ 12. Doc          L. Owns Thomas home; Mary's father

\_\_ 13. Britten      M. Mary's friend; a communist

\_\_ 14. Mr. Dalton   N. "Gang" friend of Bigger

II. Short Answer

1. Describe Bigger's relationship with his family.

2. What does Bigger mean when he says, "Half the time I feel like I'm on the outside of the world peeping in through a knot-hole in the fence..."?

*Native Son* Short Answer Unit Test 1 Page 2

3. What is Bigger saying when he tells Gus that white folks live "Right down here in my stomach"?

4. Why isn't the robbery carried out?

5. Do Jan and Mary see Bigger as a man?

6. How and why does Bigger kill Mary? What does he do with the body? Why?

7. How does Bigger feel after killing Mary?

8. Why does Bigger kill Bessie?

9. Why does Bigger reject the pleas of Rev. Hammond?

10. What had Bigger felt and caught a glimpse of for the first time in his life?

*Native Son* Short Answer Unit Test 1 Page 3

III. Composition

What is the point of *Native Son*? When we read books, we usually come away from our reading experience a little richer, having given more thought to a particular aspect of life. What do you think Richard Wright intended us to gain from reading his novel?

*Native Son* Short Answer Unit Test 1 Page 4

IV. Vocabulary
   Listen to the vocabulary words and write them down.
   Go back later and fill in the correct definition for each word.

1.

2.

3.

4.

5.

6.

7.

8.

9.

10.

# SHORT ANSWER UNIT TEST 2 - *Native Son*

I. Matching

___ 1. Peggy          A. Rich white girl

___ 2. Vera           B. Owns poolroom

___ 3. Bigger         C. State prosecutor

___ 4. Jan            D. Murders twice

___ 5. Bessie         E. Bigger's girlfriend

___ 6. Mary           F. Bigger's lawyer

___ 7. Max            G. Investigator

___ 8. Gus            H. Bigger's brother

___ 9. Buckley        I. Bigger's sister

___ 10. Mrs. Dalton   J. Mary's friend; a communist

___ 11. Buddy         K. Blind woman

___ 12. Doc           L. Owns Thomas home; Mary's father

___ 13. Britten       M. "Gang" friend of Bigger

___ 14. Mr. Dalton    N. Housekeeper

II. Short Answer

1. Why do you think Wright included the scene with the sky-writing airplane?

2. What are the two controlling emotions in Bigger's life? Give examples.

*Native Son* Short Answer Unit Test 2 Page 2

3. Do Jan and Mary see Bigger as a man?

4. How and why does Bigger kill Mary? What does he do with the body? Why?

5. To what is Wright referring when he writes, ". . . they were a sort of a great natural force, like a stormy sky looming overhead, or like a deep swirling river stretching suddenly at one's feet in the dark"?

6. Why are some of Britten's questions to Peggy concerning Bigger a bit ridiculous?

7. How does Bigger rationalize to himself that Mary and Bessie were responsible for their own deaths?

8. Why do the ping-pong tables upset Max?

9. Why is Bessie's body put on exhibition at the inquest?

*Native Son* Short Answer Unit Test 2 Page 3

III. Composition

1. Explain the significance of the title of the book *Native Son*.

2. Describe Bigger's character development through the story.

3. What different kinds of prejudice were shown in *Native Son*? Tell what kind of prejudices and give an example of each used in the book.

4. What is one major theme in the novel? How is it shown, and what is the author's viewpoint about that theme?

5. What are two major symbols in the book? For what does each stand?

*Native Son* Short Answer Unit Test 2 Page 4

IV. Vocabulary

Listen to the vocabulary words and write them down.
Go back later and fill in the correct definition for each word.

1.

2.

3.

4.

5.

6.

7.

8.

9.

10.

# KEY: SHORT ANSWER UNIT TESTS - *Native Son*

The short answer questions are taken directly from the study guides.
If you need to look up the answers, you will find them in the study guide section.

Answers to the composition questions will vary depending on your
class discussions and the level of your students.

For the vocabulary section of the test, choose ten of the
words from the vocabulary lists to read orally for your students.

The answers to the matching section of the test are below.

Answers to the matching section of the Advanced Short Answer Unit Test
are the same as for Short Answer Unit Test #2.

| Test #1 | Test #2 |
|---------|---------|
| 1. D    | 1. N    |
| 2. I    | 2. I    |
| 3. J    | 3. D    |
| 4. M    | 4. J    |
| 5. E    | 5. E    |
| 6. F    | 6. A    |
| 7. A    | 7. F    |
| 8. N    | 8. M    |
| 9. H    | 9. C    |
| 10. K   | 10. K   |
| 11. C   | 11. H   |
| 12. G   | 12. B   |
| 13. B   | 13. G   |
| 14. L   | 14. L   |

# ADVANCED SHORT ANSWER UNIT TEST - *Native Son*

I. Matching

___ 1. Peggy          A. Rich white girl

___ 2. Vera           B. Owns poolroom

___ 3. Bigger         C. State prosecutor

___ 4. Jan            D. Murders twice

___ 5. Bessie         E. Bigger's girlfriend

___ 6. Mary          F. Bigger's lawyer

___ 7. Max           G. Investigator

___ 8. Gus           H. Bigger's brother

___ 9. Buckley       I. Bigger's sister

___ 10. Mrs. Dalton   J. Mary's friend; a communist

___ 11. Buddy        K. Blind woman

___ 12. Doc          L. Owns Thomas home; Mary's father

___ 13. Britten       M. "Gang" friend of Bigger

___ 14. Mr. Dalton    N. Housekeeper

II. Short Answer

1. Discuss the significance of and give examples of dreams versus reality in *Native Son*.

*Native Son* Advanced Short Answer Unit Test Page 2

2. What are two major symbols used in *Native Son*, and for what does each stand?

3. Describe Bigger's character development throughout the novel.

4. Is Mr. Dalton a hypocrite? If so, explain how. If not, explain why not.

5. Were Mary, Jan and Max actually cruel to Bigger? If so, explain how each was. If not, explain why not.

*Native Son* Advanced Short Answer Unit Test Page 3

6. Explain how Richard Wright used Bessie in the story.

7. List at least three different kinds of prejudice that were shown in *Native Son* and give an example of each from the story.

8. Choose two characters whose relationship was most important to Richard Wright's theme development. Describe the relationship and tell why it was important.

*Native Son* Advanced Short Answer Unit Test Page 4

II. Composition

"He [Bigger] felt a sense of freedom and identity in his acts of violence that neither his woman, Bessie, with her whiskey, nor his mother, with her religion, had been able to give him."*

Explain and defend this statement as it relates to *Native Son*.

* (a quotation from the cover of the Harper and Row Publishers Perennial Library edition of *Native Son*)

*Native Son* Advanced Short Answer Unit Test Page 5

IV. Vocabulary

    Write down the vocabulary words you are given. Go back later and use all of those vocabulary words in a composition relating to *Native Son*.

# MULTIPLE CHOICE UNIT TEST 1 - *Native Son*

I. Matching/Identify

___ 1. Peggy      A. Bigger's lawyer

___ 2. Vera      B. Investigator

___ 3. Bigger      C. Bigger's brother

___ 4. Jan      D. Housekeeper

___ 5. Bessie      E. Bigger's girlfriend

___ 6. Mary      F. Rich white girl

___ 7. Max      G. Owns poolroom

___ 8. Gus      H. State prosecutor

___ 9. Buckley      I. Bigger's sister

___ 10. Mrs. Dalton      J. Murders twice

___ 11. Buddy      K. Blind woman

___ 12. Doc      L. Owns Thomas home; Mary's father

___ 13. Britten      M. Mary's friend; a communist

___ 14. Mr. Dalton      N. "Gang" friend of Bigger

II. Multiple Choice

1. Describe Bigger's relationship with his family.
   - A. He is ashamed that they have nothing and he is powerless to help them. He is resentful that they look to him for support.
   - B. He is insecure because he thinks they don't like him. He feels worthless.
   - C. He portrays an aura of confidence to make them feel better. He is especially loving towards his mother.
   - D. He is angry that he still lives with them. He despised them, especially his sister.

*Native Son* Multiple Choice Unit Test 1 Page 2

2. How does Bigger feel about his place in the world?
    A. He is content, because he doesn't know any better.
    B. He is angry, and thinks the world owes him more.
    C. He feels he is a stranger and an alien in it.
    D. He thinks he has been put on the earth for a reason, and that things will improve.

3. How did Wright show the distance between the white man's world and Bigger's?
    A. He contrasts the white and black neighborhoods.
    B. He uses billboards to show that the ads are directed to the white population of the city.
    C. He contrasts the sun outside with the darkness of the pool room.
    D. He uses the sky writing airplane to show how the white man's world is unattainable.

4. How does Bigger explain his feelings about the white folks to Gus?
    A. He says they are all liars and cheats.
    B. He says they live in his stomach; he has swallowed his anger and frustration.
    C. He says they are like poison in his blood.
    D. He says they are buzzards, preying on the weaknesses of Blacks.

5. What are the two controlling emotions in Bigger's life?
    A. They are fear and frustration.
    B. They are bewilderment and confidence.
    C. They are indifference and violence.
    D. They are optimism and pessimism.

6. How and why does Bigger kill Mary?
    A. He puts the pillow over her face to keep her quiet, and accidentally suffocates her.
    B. He decides to rob her and knifes her when she resists.
    C. He is still angry about having to eat with her and Jan, so he beats her to death.
    D. She threatens to tell her parents he attacked her, so he strangles her.

7. How does Bigger feel after killing Mary?
    A. He is still scared because now he is really in trouble with the white man's world, but he also feels a kind of pride and a direction for his life.
    B. He is remorseful, but isn't sober enough yet to think about what to do next.
    C. He is ashamed of himself and terrified at what will happen if anyone finds out what he did.
    D. He feels totally evil, but incredibly strong. He is sure he will get away with the crime.

*Native Son* Multiple Choice Unit Test 1 Page 3

8. To what is Wright referring when he writes, "...they were a sort of a great natural force, like a stormy sky looming overhead, or like a deep swirling river stretching suddenly at one's feet in the dark."?
    A. He is describing good luck and bad luck.
    B. He is describing how black people see white people.
    C. He is describing Bigger's emotions.
    D. He is describing race relations in general.

9. What does Bigger do about Bessie?
    A. He gives her money and promises to send her more as long as she keeps quiet.
    B. He leaves without telling her anything.
    C. He kills her because she is too much of a threat to him.
    D. He forces her to marry him, so that she will stay with him. In the event they are caught, she will not be able to testify against him.

10. How does Bigger deal with his actions with regards to Mary and Bessie?
    A. He prays for forgiveness, because he knows he has done terrible wrongs.
    B. He blocks both incidents from his mind so completely that he does not remember what he did.
    C. He blames them on drinking and tells himself he is not responsible for what he does when he is drunk.
    D. He thinks both women should have left him alone. They both forced him into a position where he had to do what he did.

11. Why does Bigger reject the pleas of Reverend Hammond?
    A. He doesn't believe he is worth saving.
    B. He thinks if he does as the Reverend asks he will be admitting his guilt, and may get a harsher sentence.
    C. He cannot accept that he must suffer in this world and patiently wait for death to bring happiness.
    D. He doesn't believe in God at all.

12. Why does Mr. Dalton's gesture of sending ping-pong tables to the boys' club upset Max?
    A. He thinks that Dalton is only doing it to arouse more sympathy for himself.
    B. He thinks the people who may be chosen for the jury will be influenced by the gesture.
    C. He wants Dalton to recognize that material gestures do not help the oppressed endure the suppression of their human needs.
    D. He was planning to have the communist party make the same gesture, and is irritated that Dalton beat him to it.

*Native Son* Multiple Choice Unit Test 1 Page 4

13. What does Bigger think his family and friends should feel?
    A. He thinks they should deny that they know him, to save themselves.
    B. He thinks they should be glad, and should be able to feel a part of the freedom and elation he experienced.
    C. He thinks they should be ashamed of themselves for mistreating him for so long that he was driven to commit the crimes.
    D. He thinks they should feel angry at the whites who caused his and their problems.

14. Why is Bessie's body put on exhibition at the inquest?
    A. The prosecutor wanted to try Bigger for that crime as well.
    B. It was a state law.
    C. The coroner wanted to stir up hatred and get a conviction against Bigger.
    D. The Communist Party insisted on it to show that Bigger's crime was not racially motivated.

15. How does Bigger feel after the conversation with Max?
    A. He fees even more hopeless because he realizes that since Max is also a member of a hated minority, he has little credibility with the judge and jury.
    B. He feels more relaxed than he has ever felt before, free of much of the strain and stress that has controlled him.
    C. He accepts the responsibility of his actions, and feels resigned to his fate.
    D. He thinks of Max as just another lying white man, and he doesn't trust him.

*Native Son* Multiple Choice Unit Test 1 Page 5

III. Composition

What motivates Bigger Thomas to do what he does? What is the root cause of his actions? Explain thoroughly using examples from the book to support your statements.

*Native Son* Multiple Choice Unit Test 1 Page 6

IV. Vocabulary - Match the correct definitions to the words.

___ 1. Taut              a. Wrong; not within accepted guidelines

___ 2. Rendered          b. Something that hinders, engulfs, or overwhelms

___ 3. Exhorted          c. Urged through arguments and appeals

___ 4. Endure            d. Promised

___ 5. Peeved            e. Tense; tight

___ 6. Indelible         f. Carry on through hardships

___ 7. Foreboding        g. Enthusiastically; fervently

___ 8. Duped             h. Deceived; made foolish

___ 9. Ardently          i. Permanent

___ 10. Conjectured      j. Anxiously; fearfully

___ 11. Inarticulate     k. Give in; come under the influence of

___ 12. Succumb          l. Leeway; freedom within regulations

___ 13. Latitude         m. Made; caused to be

___ 14. Vowed            n. Overbearingly, pressingly, urgently

___ 15. Apprehensively   o. Dormant; present but not evident or active

___ 16. Unethical        p. Thought; came to a conclusion based on present evidence

___ 17. Morass           q. Predicting something bad for the future

___ 18. Imperiously      r. Wordless; speechless

___ 19. Condemned        s. Vexed; angry

___ 20. Latent           t. Found guilty or unfit

# MULTIPLE CHOICE UNIT TEST 2 - *Native Son*

I. Matching

___ 1. Peggy           A. Rich white girl

___ 2. Vera            B. Owns poolroom

___ 3. Bigger          C. State prosecutor

___ 4. Jan             D. Murders twice

___ 5. Bessie          E. Bigger's girlfriend

___ 6. Mary            F. Bigger's lawyer

___ 7. Max             G. Investigator

___ 8. Gus             H. Bigger's brother

___ 9. Buckley         I. Bigger's sister

___ 10. Mrs. Dalton    J. Mary's friend; a communist

___ 11. Buddy          K. Blind woman

___ 12. Doc            L. Owns Thomas home; Mary's father

___ 13. Britten        M. "Gang" friend of Bigger

___ 14. Mr. Dalton     N. Housekeeper

II. Multiple Choice
1. Describe Bigger's relationship with his family.
    A. He is insecure because he thinks they don't like him. He feels worthless.
    B. He is ashamed that they have nothing and he is powerless to help them. He is resentful that they look to him for support.
    C. He portrays an aura of confidence to make them feel better. He is especially loving towards his mother.
    D. He is angry that he still lives with them. He despised them, especially his sister.

*Native Son* Multiple Choice Unit Test 2 Page 2

2. How does Bigger feel about his place in the world?
   A. He is content, because he doesn't know any better.
   B. He is angry, and thinks the world owes him more.
   C. He thinks he has been put on the earth for a reason, and that things will improve.
   D. He feels he is a stranger and an alien in it.

3. How did Wright show the distance between the white man's world and Bigger's?
   A. He contrasts the white and black neighborhoods.
   B. He uses billboards to show that the ads are directed to the white population of the city.
   C. He uses the sky writing airplane to show how the white man's world is unattainable.
   D. He contrasts the sun outside with the darkness of the pool room.

4. How does Bigger explain his feelings about the white folks to Gus?
   A. He says they live in his stomach; he has swallowed his anger and frustration.
   B. He says they are all liars and cheats.
   C. He says they are like poison in his blood.
   D. He says they are buzzards, preying on the weaknesses of Blacks.

5. What are the two controlling emotions in Bigger's life?
   A. They are fear and frustration.
   B. They are indifference and violence.
   C. They are bewilderment and confidence.
   D. They are optimism and pessimism.

6. How and why does Bigger kill Mary?
   A. He is still angry about having to eat with her and Jan, so he beats her to death.
   B. He decides to rob her and knifes her when she resists.
   C. He puts the pillow over her face to keep her quiet, and accidentally suffocates her.
   D. She threatens to tell her parents he attacked her, so he strangles her.

7. How does Bigger feel after killing Mary?
   A. He feels totally evil, but incredibly strong. He is sure he will get away with the crime.
   B. He is remorseful, but isn't sober enough yet to think about what to do next.
   C. He is ashamed of himself and terrified at what will happen if anyone finds out what he did.
   D. He is still scared because now he is really in trouble with the white man's world, but he also feels a kind of pride and a direction for his life.

*Native Son* Multiple Choice Unit Test 2 Page 3

8. To what is Wright referring when he writes, "...they were a sort of a great natural force, like a stormy sky looming overhead, or like a deep swirling river stretching suddenly at one's feet in the dark."?
    A. He is describing how black people see white people.
    B. He is describing good luck and bad luck.
    C. He is describing Bigger's emotions.
    D. He is describing race relations in general.

9. What does Bigger do about Bessie?
    A. He gives her money and promises to send her more as long as she keeps quiet.
    B. He leaves without telling her anything.
    C. He forces her to marry him, so that she will stay with him. In the event they are caught, she will not be able to testify against him.
    D. He kills her because she is too much of a threat to him.

10. How does Bigger deal with his actions with regards to Mary and Bessie?
    A. He thinks both women should have left him alone. They both forced him into a position where he had to do what he did.
    B. He blocks both incidents from his mind so completely that he does not remember what he did.
    C. He blames them on drinking and tells himself he is not responsible for what he does when he is drunk.
    D. He prays for forgiveness, because he knows he has done terrible wrongs.

11. Why does Bigger reject the pleas of Reverend Hammond?
    A. He doesn't believe he is worth saving.
    B. He cannot accept that he must suffer in this world and patiently wait for death to bring happiness.
    C. He thinks if he does as the Reverend asks he will be admitting his guilt, and may get a harsher sentence.
    D. He doesn't believe in God at all.

12. Why does Mr. Dalton's gesture of sending ping-pong tables to the boys' club upset Max?
    A. He thinks that Dalton is only doing it to arouse more sympathy for himself.
    B. He thinks the people who may be chosen for the jury will be influenced by the gesture.
    C. He was planning to have the communist party make the same gesture, and is irritated that Dalton beat him to it.
    D. He wants Dalton to recognize that material gestures do not help the oppressed endure the suppression of their human needs.

*Native Son* Multiple Choice Unit Test 2 Page 4

13. What does Bigger think his family and friends should feel?
    A. He thinks they should be glad, and should be able to feel a part of the freedom and elation he experienced.
    B. He thinks they should deny that they know him, to save themselves.
    C. He thinks they should be ashamed of themselves for mistreating him for so long that he was driven to commit the crimes.
    D. He thinks they should feel angry at the whites who caused his and their problems.

14. Why is Bessie's body put on exhibition at the inquest?
    A. The coroner wanted to stir up hatred and get a conviction against Bigger.
    B. It was a state law.
    C. The prosecutor wanted to try Bigger for that crime as well.
    D. The Communist Party insisted on it to show that Bigger's crime was not racially motivated.

15. How does Bigger feel after the conversation with Max?
    A. He accepts the responsibility of his actions, and feels resigned to his fate.
    B. He feels more relaxed than he has ever felt before, free of much of the strain and stress that has controlled him.
    C. He fees even more hopeless because he realizes that since Max is also a member of a hated minority, he has little credibility with the judge and jury.
    D. He thinks of Max as just another lying white man, and he doesn't trust him.

III. Composition

    Most books have a "good guy" and a "bad guy." Does this book have those elements? If so, explain who fills each role and why. If not, explain why these elements are not present in this book.

*Native Son* Multiple Choice Unit Test 2 Page 6

IV. Vocabulary - Match the correct definitions to the words.

___ 1. Contrite          a. Made; caused to be

___ 2. Aspiration        b. Anxiously; fearfully

___ 3. Apprehensively    c. Predicting something bad for the future

___ 4. Anarchist         d. Hostilely

___ 5. Contagion         e. Deceived; made foolish

___ 6. Belligerently     f. Remaining, as though reluctant to leave

___ 7. Sullen            g. Found guilty or unfit

___ 8. Morass            h. Something that hinders, engulfs, or overwhelms

___ 9. Consented         i. Agreement

___ 10. Mitigating       j. Wordless; speechless

___ 11. Lulled           k. Sulky

___ 12. Duped            l. One who is against all forms of government

___ 13. Queer            m. Agreed

___ 14. Condemned        n. Calmed

___ 15. Flaccid          o. Strange

___ 16. Rendered         p. Sorry for past actions

___ 17. Accord           q. Making more moderate

___ 18. Foreboding       r. Lacking firmness or muscle tone

___ 19. Lingering        s. Easily transmitted disease

___ 20. Inarticulate     t. Ambition

## ANSWER SHEET - *Native Son*
## Multiple Choice Unit Tests

I. Matching
1. ___
2. ___
3. ___
4. ___
5. ___
6. ___
7. ___
8. ___
9. ___
10. ___
11. ___
12. ___
13. ___
14. ___

II. Multiple Choice
1. ___
2. ___
3. ___
4. ___
5. ___
6. ___
7. ___
8. ___
9. ___
10. ___
11. ___
12. ___
13. ___
14. ___
15. ___

IV. Vocabulary
1. ___
2. ___
3. ___
4. ___
5. ___
6. ___
7. ___
8. ___
9. ___
10. ___
11. ___
12. ___
13. ___
14. ___
15. ___
16. ___
17. ___
18. ___
19. ___
20. ___

ANSWER KEY - *Native Son*
Multiple Choice Unit Tests

Answers to Unit Test 1 are in the left column. Answers to Unit Test 2 are in the right column.

| I. Matching | II. Multiple Choice | IV. Vocabulary |
|---|---|---|
| 1. D   N | 1. A   B | 1. E   P |
| 2. I   I | 2. C   D | 2. M   T |
| 3. J   D | 3. D   C | 3. C   B |
| 4. M   J | 4. B   A | 4. F   L |
| 5. E   E | 5. C   B | 5. S   S |
| 6. F   A | 6. A   C | 6. I   D |
| 7. A   F | 7. A   D | 7. Q   K |
| 8. N   M | 8. B   A | 8. H   H |
| 9. H   C | 9. C   D | 9. G   M |
| 10. K   K | 10. D   A | 10. P   Q |
| 11. C   H | 11. C   B | 11. R   N |
| 12. G   B | 12. C   D | 12. K   E |
| 13. B   G | 13. B   A | 13. L   O |
| 14. L   L | 14. C   A | 14. D   G |
|  | 15. B   B | 15. J   R |
|  |  | 16. A   A |
|  |  | 17. B   I |
|  |  | 18. N   C |
|  |  | 19. T   F |
|  |  | 20. O   J |

# UNIT RESOURCE MATERIALS

# BULLETIN BOARD IDEAS - *Native Son*

1. Save one corner of the board for the best of students' *Native Son* writing assignments.

2. Take one of the word search puzzles from the extra activities packet and with a marker copy it over in a large size on the bulletin board. Write the clue words to find to one side. Invite students prior to and after class to find the words and circle them on the bulletin board.

3. Write several of the most significant quotations from the book onto the board on brightly colored paper.

4. Make a bulletin board listing the vocabulary words for this unit. As you complete sections of the novel and discuss the vocabulary for each section, write the definitions on the bulletin board. (If your board is one students face frequently, it will help them learn the words.)

5. Do a bulletin board about ways to deal with stress, anger and frustration.

6. Use the bulletin board suggested in the introductory lesson.

7. Make a bulletin board about the history of the Civil Rights Movement.

8. Make a bulletin board on which you post pictures and short biographies of famous black authors, including Richard Wright.

9. Have students make an event time line of the story and use the bulletin board for this activity.

10. Have students make a bulletin board about fear. Have each student bring in a picture (or anything that can be posted on the bulletin board) that represents something that makes us afraid. Use this bulletin board as a springboard for a discussion of fears and how to cope with them.

# EXTRA ACTIVITIES - *Native Son*

One of the difficulties in teaching a novel is that all students don't read at the same speed. One student who likes to read may take the book home and finish it in a day or two. Sometimes a few students finish the in-class assignments early. The problem, then, is finding suitable extra activities for students.

The best thing I've found is to keep a little library in the classroom. For this unit on *Native Son,* you might check out from the school library other related books and articles about the civil rights movement, our justice system, careers in the justice system, the history of Communism in America, or information about coping with stress and anger. Other books by or a biography about Richard Wright would be helpful. Also consider articles of criticism about *Native Son.*

Other things you may keep on hand are puzzles. We have made some relating directly to *Native Son* for you. Feel free to duplicate them.

Some students may like to draw. You might devise a contest or allow some extra-credit grade for students who draw characters or scenes from *Native Son.* Note, too, that if the students do not want to keep their drawings you may pick up some extra bulletin board materials this way. If you have a contest and you supply the prize (a record album or something like that perhaps), you could, possibly, make the drawing itself a non-returnable entry fee.

The pages which follow contain games, puzzles and worksheets. The keys, when appropriate, immediately follow the puzzle or worksheet. There are two main groups of activities: one group for the unit; that is, generally relating to the *Native Son* text, and another group of activities related strictly to the *Native Son* vocabulary.

Directions for these games, puzzles and worksheets are self-explanatory. The object here is to provide you with extra materials you may use in any way you choose.

# MORE ACTIVITIES - *Native Son*

1. Pick a chapter or scene with a great deal of dialogue and have the students act it out on a stage. (Perhaps you could assign various scenes to different groups of students so more than one scene could be acted and more students could participate.)

2. Have students design a book cover (front and back and inside flaps) for *Native Son.*

3. Have students design a bulletin board (ready to be put up; not just sketched) for *Native Son.*

4. Use some of the related topics noted earlier for an in-class library as topics for research, reports or written papers, or as topics for guest speakers.

5. Take a field trip to see your local jail or courtrooms. Take time to watch a trial if one is scheduled.

6. Have your students create their own version of Bigger's trial and come to their own conclusions. Involve the whole class as judge, attorneys, jurors, witnesses, members of the press, etc.

7. Have students read another work of fiction that deals with the same theme(s) as *Native Son* and have students compare the work they read to *Native Son.*

8. After students complete their nonfiction reading project, generate a list of the problems facing black Americans today. Have students meet in small groups to brainstorm effective ways of overcoming the problems.

9. Like Richard Wright, many authors in the period from 1920-1940 went to Europe to live -- or frequently visited there. Have students research who went there and why they went.

10. Have a group project surrounding the city of Chicago. Assign different aspects of the city's history and culture to each group of students. Topics could include history, shopping, sights to see, economy, etc.

# WORD SEARCH - *Native Son*

All words in this list are associated with *Native Son*. The words are placed backwards, forward, diagonally, up and down. The included words are listed below the word searches.

```
R Y Q X J M L N H Y X N Z L T M G N F K H P F F
M A G L N S D W M D H N M R N M K N A W N V A L
W L P U C X E J E R W T U M E Z Y B O R V T Z C
A S H E S T O M A C H O U T S I D E R P E G G Y
R C L O V R A E O G C L L P H O S E L I G V T Z
Q L N Q N H F W I S B J L L C G G S R K T N L D
H N X M S W L L C F N W A Y I G I S E N C T I W
M A H A A B F N O T L A D N I P H R E B L U E P
M Y M B V R L D Z Z P D R B R P F C W V J V B N
S N J M J T Y I H K U T V E T H A T T I K T L
R V Z Q O N R P N B Y K J S B N V T B T X V W F
J V W Z Q N Y P B D W U K K R X P S A K H P S J
K F C W L X D D V Z D V G U B J P N X K B X M K
Y W S P T F S J N I N L F V G Y Y H T C R V B B
H T V G H B Q W C K X V F F K F D Z W J T T W Z
W F V S Y C Q E S Z B B H R J F L N T F M L H Z
F J D B C B Z D Y M J Y S G D N S H Y D M R M F
```

| | | | |
|---|---|---|---|
| ASHAMED | CELL | HAMMOND | PREJUDICE |
| ASHES | COURT | JAN | RANSOM |
| BESSIE | DALTON | MARY | RAPE |
| BIGGER | DOC | MAX | SON |
| BLIND | FATE | NATIVE | STOMACH |
| BLUM | FEAR | OUTSIDE | VERA |
| BRITTEN | FLIGHT | PEGGY | WRIGHT |
| BUCKLEY | FURNACE | PILLOW | BUDDY |
| GUS | PINGPONG | | |

# CROSSWORD - *Native Son*

# CROSSWORD CLUES - *Native Son*

**ACROSS**

2. These were the rhythms of his life: --- and violence
9. Mary's --- was covered so she couldn't breathe
10. Mr. ---; owns Thomas home; Mary's father
11. Bigger's initials
12. Bigger's girlfriend
13. Book I title
15. Murders twice
17. Remain
18. Mary's friend; a communist
20. Owns poolroom
21. Bigger feels --- and resentful when he is with his family
25. Murder weapon in Mary's murder
26. Trial room
27. Out of danger
29. Native ---
30. Bigger's lawyer
32. Housekeeper
34. Preacher from Bigger's mother's church
35. Bigger was charged with the --- and murder of Mary
39. Preconceived idea
41. Author
42. Bother

**DOWN**

1. Bigger's brother
3. ----- Son
4. Book III title
5. Slang for Communists
6. Mary and Jan thought they were being ---- to Bigger
7. The last word on the last page. There is no more.
8. The evidence that lead to Bigger's downfall
11. Investigator
14. Bigger's sister
15. State prosecutor
16. Gang friend of Bigger
19. Rich white girl who is murdered
22. White folks live right down here in my ----
23. Bigger, Gus, Jack and GH plan to rob ----'s Store
24. Half the time I feel like I'm on the -- of the world peeping in
25. Mr. Dalton sent these tables to the boys' club
26. Jail room
28. Where Bigger put Mary's body
31. In the middle of
33. Leave
36. Church seats
37. The guard brought the key to --- the cell door for the preacher
38. Belonging to it
40. Happiness

## CROSSWORD ANSWER KEY - *Native Son*

# MATCHING QUIZ/WORKSHEET 1 - *Native Son*

___ 1. FLIGHT          A. Bigger plans to get $10,000 from Mr. Dalton as --- money

___ 2. STOMACH         B. Bigger's girlfriend

___ 3. NATIVE          C. Bigger's brother

___ 4. PING PONG       D. The evidence that lead to Bigger's downfall

___ 5. VERA            E. Mr. Dalton sent these tables to the boys' club

___ 6. BESSIE          F. Bigger feels --- and resentful when he is with his family

___ 7. PEGGY           G. Mrs. Dalton's handicap

___ 8. DOC             H. Bigger's sister

___ 9. MARY            I. Preacher from Bigger's mother's church

___ 10. BUDDY          J. Owns poolroom

___ 11. MAX            K. Bigger's lawyer

___ 12. ASHES          L. Housekeeper

___ 13. ASHAMED        M. White folks live right down here in my ----

___ 14. RANSOM         N. Book III title

___ 15. BLIND          O. Preconceived idea

___ 16. FATE           P. Rich white girl who is murdered

___ 17. PILLOW         Q. Book II title

___ 18. HAMMOND        R. Murder weapon in Mary's murder

___ 19. PREJUDICE      S. Investigator

___ 20. BRITTEN        T. ----- Son

# MATCHING QUIZ/WORKSHEET 2 - *Native Son*

___ 1. RANSOM         A. Bigger's brother

___ 2. FURNACE        B. Preacher from Bigger's mother's church

___ 3. HAMMOND        C. Half the time I feel like I'm on the -- of the world peeping in

___ 4. FATE           D. Where Bigger put Mary's body

___ 5. JAN            E. Investigator

___ 6. DALTON         F. Bigger plans to get $10,000 from Mr. Dalton as --- money

___ 7. CELL           G. Book II title

___ 8. RAPE           H. Bigger's lawyer

___ 9. BUDDY          I. Murder weapon in Mary's murder

___ 10. BLUM          J. State prosecutor

___ 11. MAX           K. Bigger was charged with the --- and murder of Mary

___ 12. PILLOW        L. Bigger feels --- and resentful when he is with his family

___ 13. PEGGY         M. Mr. ---; owns Thomas home; Mary's father

___ 14. FLIGHT        N. Bigger, Gus, Jack and GH plan to rob ----'s Store

___ 15. BUCKLEY       O. Native ---

___ 16. SON           P. Housekeeper

___ 17. PREJUDICE     Q. Book III title

___ 18. ASHAMED       R. Mary's friend; a communist

___ 19. BRITTEN       S. Jail room

___ 20. OUTSIDE       T. Preconceived idea

## KEY: MATCHING QUIZ/WORKSHEETS - *Native Son*

| Worksheet 1 | Worksheet 2 |
|---|---|
| 1. Q | 1. F |
| 2. M | 2. D |
| 3. T | 3. B |
| 4. E | 4. Q |
| 5. H | 5. R |
| 6. B | 6. M |
| 7. L | 7. S |
| 8. J | 8. K |
| 9. P | 9. A |
| 10. C | 10. N |
| 11. K | 11. H |
| 12. D | 12. I |
| 13. F | 13. P |
| 14. A | 14. G |
| 15. G | 15. J |
| 16. N | 16. O |
| 17. R | 17. T |
| 18. I | 18. L |
| 19. O | 19. E |
| 20. S | 20. C |

# JUGGLE LETTER REVIEW GAME CLUE SHEET - *Native Son*

| SCRAMBLED | WORD | CLUE |
|---|---|---|
| LOWPIL | PILLOW | Murder weapon in Mary's murder |
| CDUEEJRPI | PREJUDICE | Preconceived idea |
| GPYEG | PEGGY | Housekeeper |
| MUBL | BLUM | Bigger, Gus, Jack and GH plan to rob ____'s Store |
| LHTFIG | FLIGHT | Book II title |
| TNREITB | BRITTEN | Investigator |
| ANJ | JAN | Mary's friend; a communist |
| CDO | DOC | Owns poolroom |
| SGU | GUS | Gang friend of Bigger |
| SIEBES | BESSIE | Bigger's girlfriend |
| RVAE | VERA | Bigger's sister |
| UACERNF | FURNACE | Where Bigger put Mary's body |
| TFEA | FATE | Book III title |
| LLEC | CELL | Jail room |
| YRMA | MARY | Rich white girl who is murdered |
| PERA | RAPE | Bigger was charged with the ____ and murder of Mary |
| TGRIWH | WRIGHT | Author |
| NSO | SON | Native _____ |
| AVINET | NATIVE | _____ Son |
| SHESA | ASHES | The evidence that lead to Bigger's downfall |
| CBEUYLK | BUCKLEY | State prosecutor |
| YDBUD | BUDDY | Bigger's brother |
| ARFE | FEAR | Book I title |
| UISTOED | OUTSIDE | Half the time I feel like I'm on the _____ of the world peeping in |
| MHANDOM | HAMMOND | Preacher from Bigger's mother's church |
| REGBGI | BIGGER | Murders twice |
| AXM | MAX | Bigger's lawyer |
| FRINCNFEEEID | INDIFFERENCE | These were the rhythms of his life; _____ and violence |
| NOTLDA | DALTON | Mr. ____; owns Thomas home; Mary's father |
| EASDAMH | ASHAMED | Bigger feels ____ and resentful when he is with his family |
| ASRMNO | RANSOM | Bigger plans to get $10,000 from Mr. Dalton as _____ money |

# VOCABULARY RESOURCE MATERIALS

# VOCABULARY WORD SEARCH - *Native Son*

All words in this list are associated with *Native Son* with an emphasis on the vocabulary words chosen for study in the text. The words are placed backwards, forward, diagonally, up and down. The included words are listed below.

```
Z Q B P N Q S A L T T R H E E G N I R E G N I L
T Y D J E O W S J N L C K C L S Y O T X S D P P
F U T I L E I N E X T R I C A B L Y I R K E D N
Y O A N C Z V T D I J N W R M O A U L T E Q D C
G E R T E C A E A T T M E U R U R P P R C E L Z
E R A E V L A E D R L N C M I E N P L M U N U P
R X A R B E O L L P I C A M N M V E E A I S A Q
Y E H T N O N V F A U P O L T G P O T R P M D S
D L N O I I D U E S T R S N I X I U C H U M B Z
F E T D R F N I E N A I D A T G Y A T A I D I Q
G A L N E T Y G N S E E O N L R I N R E B C N W
F S Y L E R E L S G B B A N D I I V D R D L A E
S T A V E D E D U B Q M E D C R B T O Y A C E L
P V X J E P R D E L R L L X Y M O I E W X W N X
R M D P C J M A Z O L S K B S W M C J D E K W H
E L U D E D D I D U V E A B S T R A C T E D L Y
E D U T I T A L S T Q L D I M P L I C A T E M D
```

| | | | |
|---|---|---|---|
| ABSTRACTEDLY | ELATION | INEXTRICABLY | SANCTION |
| ACCORD | ELUDED | IRKED | STAVE |
| ALIBI | ENDURE | IRREVOCABLE | SUCCUMB |
| ARDENTLY | EXHORTED | LABYRINTH | SULLEN |
| ARRAIGNMENT | FLACCID | LATENT | SURLY |
| ASPIRATION | FOREBODING | LATITUDE | TAUT |
| ATONE | FUTILE | LINGERING | UNETHICAL |
| AWE | GRATIFY | LULLED | VENUE |
| BENEVOLENT | IMPALPABLE | MORASS | VIGILANTES |
| CONTRITE | IMPELLED | PEEVED | VOWED |
| DORMANT | IMPLICATE | QUEER | YEARNING |
| DUPED | IMPULSE | RENDERED | |
| EBBED | IMPUTED | REPROACH | |

# VOCABULARY CROSSWORD - *Native Son*

# VOCABULARY CROSSWORD CLUES - *Native Son*

ACROSS
2. Motivated; had the feeling of needing to do something
4. Suggestive of doing good
7. Strange
8. Mary ---d
9. Tense; tight
11. Useless
12. Definite article
14. Having the power to decide
16. Foreign; dissimilar; strange
17. To flow away from
18. Make a mistake
23. Hostilely
25. Mary's friend; a communist
26. Gang friend of Bigger
27. Deceived; made foolish
28. Agreement
30. Not clear; lacking a definite shape
32. High point
33. Bad-humored; gruff
38. Vexed; angry
40. Sight organ
41. Action
42. Asleep; inactive
44. A threesome
47. Put off; postpone
48. Book I title
50. Book III title
51. Quieted; settled
52. Bigger was the --- of Mary and Jan at the restaurant

DOWN
1. A motion of the limbs or body as an expression of thought or for emphasis
2. Irritated; bothered
3. Tell an untruth
4. Make known unintentionally
5. Escaped from one's understanding
6. Calmed
7. Trembling
8. Owns poolroom
10. A mixed emotion of reverence, respect and dread
13. Feeling indignant ill-will
15. Sulky
19. In a manner apart from the situation
20. Location (city, state) where a trial is held
21. Carry on through hardships
22. Changed
24. Inclination; motivating force
26. Satisfy; indulge
29. Agreed
30. Promised
31. Grabbed
34. Made; caused to be
35. Longing
36. Turned away
37. Something that hinders, engulfs, or overwhelms
39. Making a low, dull humming noise
43. Make up for; make amends for
45. Rich white girl who is murdered
46. Bigger's lawyer
49. That's all; there is no more

# VOCABULARY CROSSWORD ANSWER KEY - *Native Son*

A completed crossword puzzle grid containing the following words:

Across and down entries visible in the grid include: GIMPELLED (IMPELLED), BENEVOLENT, QUEER, DIE, TAUT, FUTILE, THE, DECISIVE, ALIEN, EBBED, ERR, BELLIGERENTLY, JAN, GUS, DUPED, ACCORD, VAGUE, PINNACLE, SURLY, PEEVED, DEED, DORMANT, TRIO, STAVE, FEAR, FATE, SUBSIDED, GUEST.

# VOCABULARY WORKSHEET 1 - *Native Son*

___ 1. YEARNING	A. Make up for; make amends for

___ 2. MORASS	B. Longing

___ 3. TAUT	C. To flow away from

___ 4. PREMEDITATION	D. Something that hinders, engulfs, or overwhelms

___ 5. LINGERING	E. Dormant; present but not evident or active

___ 6. HYSTERICAL	F. Planning beforehand

___ 7. IRREVOCABLE	G. Added to; supplemented

___ 8. AUGMENTED	H. Tense; tight

___ 9. ATONE	I. Lacking firmness or muscle tone

___ 10. EBBED	J. Maze

___ 11. LATENT	K. Wordless; speechless

___ 12. FUTILE	L. Hostilely

___ 13. GRATIFY	M. Deceived; made foolish

___ 14. IMPUTED	N. Remaining, as though reluctant to leave

___ 15. ASPIRATION	O. Satisfy; indulge

___ 16. FLACCID	P. Having uncontrolled emotions

___ 17. INARTICULATE	Q. Attributed; credited

___ 18. DUPED	R. Can't be taken back or sent back

___ 19. BELLIGERENTLY	S. Ambition

___ 20. LABYRINTH	T. Useless

# VOCABULARY WORKSHEET 2 - *Native Son*

___ 1. Attributed; credited
    a. Sullen     b. Arraignment     c. Gratify     d. Imputed

___ 2. Remaining, as though reluctant to leave
    a. Venue     b. Yearning     c. Lingering     d. Ebbed

___ 3. Hostilely
    a. Belligerently     b. Conjectured     c. Inarticulate     d. Implicate

___ 4. Satisfy; indulge
    a. Subsided     b. Accord     c. Gratify     d. Conjectured

___ 5. Added to; supplemented
    a. Aspiration     b. Arraignment     c. Augmented     d. Condemned

___ 6. Lacking firmness or muscle tone
    a. Vigilantes     b. Flaccid     c. Aspiration     d. Stave

___ 7. Making more moderate
    a. Vigilantes     b. Contrite     c. Mitigating     d. Eluded

___ 8. Anxiously; fearfully
    a. Subsided     b. Vigilantes     c. Apprehensively     d. Contrite

___ 9. Leeway; freedom within regulations
    a. Latitude     b. Ardently     c. Sullen     d. Anarchist

___ 10. Give in; come under the influence of
    a. Flaccid     b. Impulse     c. Succumb     d. Consented

___ 11. Dormant; present but not evident or active
    a. Latent     b. Succumb     c. Taut     d. Foreboding

___ 12. Disapproval
    a. Dormant     b. Vigilantes     c. Morass     d. Reproach

___ 13. A mixed emotion of reverence, respect and dread
    a. Condemned     b. Latitude     c. Belligerently     d. Awe

___ 14. Made; caused to be
    a. Imperiously     b. Rendered     c. Ebbed     d. Succumb

___ 15. Ambition
    a. Aspiration     b. Conjectured     c. Impelled     d. Queer

___ 16. Promised
    a. Premeditation     b. Impulse     c. Duped     d. Vowed

___ 17. Found guilty or unfit
    a. Rendered     b. Accord     c. Condemned     d. Dormant

___ 18. Overbearingly, pressingly, urgently
    a. Lingering     b. Gratify     c. Venue     d. Imperiously

___ 19. Suggestive of doing good
    a. Venue     b. Eluded     c. Benevolent     d. Condemned

___ 20. Feeling of extreme happiness or pleasure
    a. Inextricably     b. Futile     c. Elation     d. Indelible

# KEY: VOCABULARY WORKSHEETS - *Native Son*

| Worksheet 1 | Worksheet 2 |
|---|---|
| 1. B | 1. D |
| 2. D | 2. C |
| 3. H | 3. A |
| 4. F | 4. C |
| 5. N | 5. C |
| 6. P | 6. B |
| 7. R | 7. C |
| 8. G | 8. C |
| 9. A | 9. A |
| 10. C | 10. C |
| 11. E | 11. A |
| 12. T | 12. D |
| 13. O | 13. D |
| 14. Q | 14. B |
| 15. S | 15. A |
| 16. I | 16. D |
| 17. K | 17. C |
| 18. M | 18. D |
| 19. L | 19. C |
| 20. J | 20. C |

## VOCABULARY JUGGLE LETTER REVIEW GAME CLUES - *Native Son*

| SCRAMBLED | WORD | CLUE |
| --- | --- | --- |
| RHELYCTASI | HYSTERICAL | Having uncontrolled emotions |
| ONIGNOCTA | CONTAGION | Easily transmitted disease |
| DSUISEDB | SUBSIDED | Quieted; settled |
| SLOIYUREPMI | IMPERIOUSLY | Overbearingly, pressingly, urgently |
| BLTSAYADRTEC | ABSTRACTEDLY | In a manner apart from the situation |
| MIEIATPLC | IMPLICATE | Connect incriminatingly |
| CLNAETUHI | UNETHICAL | Wrong; not within accepted guidelines |
| TJDECCNRUOE | CONJECTURED | Thought; came to a conclusion based on present evidence |
| IIBAL | ALIBI | An excuse; a way to prove one could not have committed a crime |
| NAMIGRNATER | ARRAIGNMENT | To call an accused person to court to answer the charges against him/her |
| RLSUY | SURLY | Bad-humored; gruff |
| ACTUIEIRATLN | INARTICULATE | Wordless; speechless |
| DEDELU | ELUDED | Escaped from one's understanding |
| TOSNARIIAP | ASPIRATION | Ambition |
| GLGERININ | LINGERING | Remaining, as though reluctant to leave |
| VSTEA | STAVE | Put off; postpone |
| EVDWO | VOWED | Promised |
| EBDBE | EBBED | To flow away from |
| LLSENU | SULLEN | Sulky |
| LEDULL | LULLED | Calmed |
| UEREQ | QUEER | Strange |
| ONTEA | ATONE | Make up for; make amends for |
| DIEELLPM | IMPELLED | Motivated; had the feeling of needing to do something |
| ERGINYBLLELTE | BELLIGERENTLY | Hostilely |
| VEBIERLRCAO | IRREVOCABLE | Can't be taken back or sent back |
| ORCEPHRA | REPROACH | Disapproval |
| ATNEOIL | ELATION | Feeling of extreme happiness or pleasure |
| EEODNNSTC | CONSENTED | Agreed |
| IANGANUTB | UNABATING | Not subsiding; not becoming less |
| NROCETIT | CONTRITE | Sorry for past actions |
| TTIDEAUL | LATITUDE | Leeway; freedom within regulations |
| DTMTNAIEPEORI | PREMEDITATION | Planning beforehand |
| KIRDE | IRKED | Irritated; bothered |
| INTRLHBAY | LABYRINTH | Maze |
| EGDUEAMNT | AUGMENTED | Added to; supplemented |

| | | |
|---|---|---|
| CCUUSBM | SUCCUMB | Give in; come under the influence of |
| TELYHCAISR | HYSTERICAL | Having uncontrolled emotions |
| NRINAYGE | YEARNING | Longing |
| AUTT | TAUT | Tense; tight |
| ONCNMDEDE | CONDEMNED | Found guilty or unfit |
| UTELFI | FUTILE | Useless |
| WEA | AWE | A mixed emotion of reverence, respect and dread |
| GALITEISNV | VIGILANTES | People who take the law into their own hands |
| TEUDPMI | IMPUTED | Attributed; credited |
| DEUDP | DUPED | Deceived; made foolish |

www.ingramcontent.com/pod-product-compliance
Lightning Source LLC
Chambersburg PA
CBHW051418070526
44584CB00023B/3479